WWW.LANNOO.COM

Register on our website and we will regularly send you a newsletter with information about our latest books as well as interesting, exclusive offers.

Text: Frank Fol, Ilse De Vis
Recipes: Frank Fol
Photography: Wim Demessemaekers, The Soul Food Photographer
Graphic Design: Studio Lannoo (Aurelie Matthys)
Graphic Design Cover: Ilse De Vis
Typesetting: Keppie & Keppie

If you have any comments or questions, please contact our editors:
redactielifestyle@lannoo.com

© Frank Fol, Ilse De Vis & Uitgeverij Lannoo nv, Tielt, 2021
D/2021/45/548 – NUR 440, 441
ISBN: 9789401480093

All rights reserved. Nothing from this edition may be reproduced, recorded in an automated database and/or published in any form or in any way, whether electronic, mechanical or in any other manner without the prior written permission of the publisher.

WILD COOKING

SURPRISING SEASONAL DISHES WITH FRESH VEGETABLES AND FRUIT

ILSE DE VIS & FRANK FOL
PHOTOGRAPHY: WIM DEMESSEMAEKERS

Lannoo

CONTENTS

SPRING

Stir-fried cauliflower and turnip greens with Greek yogurt and oatmeal	24
Watermelon-lime drink with mint	24
Crackers with carrot salad and Kikuna Leaves	25
Fresh water with celery and Motti Cress	25
Grilled toast with apple-tomato marmalade, truffle dust and Floregano	29
Cucumber gazpacho with kefir and Melissa Cress	30
Smaakbom® salsa with Légumaise Thai and Ghoa Cress	34
BBQ croque radish with mushroom and truffle Légumaise and Garden Cress	37
Pea soup with lemon balm, fried shallots, sweet potato and sea fennel	41
Finger food: Shiso Leaves Green with a celery, tomato, egg mimosa and white truffle oil spread	42
BBQ shallot "oysters" with potato, raspberry and Limon Cress	46
Chard-peach pillows with grilled chard sticks, chermoula and Vene Cress	51
Cabbage wushi with quinoa, mitsuna lettuce, Thai basil, black sesame and Légumaise Thai	57
Asparagus spaghetti with potato straws, caviar and RucolaCress	58
BBQ pointed cabbage steak with radish sauce, cashew nuts, argan oil and Kyona Mustard Cress	61
Braised turnips with redcurrant, tempranillo, gomasio and Mustard Cress	64
Ripe pear and fennel carpaccio, pink grapefruit, pistachio, goji berry and Yka Leaves	67
Grilled honey-lacquered rhubarb, ginger nut crumble, olive ice cream and Honny Cress	71
Strawberry-rhubarb sweet with lemon and Paztizz Tops	72
Cauliflower slices with crema di tartufi bianchi and Persinette + Raw asparagus curls with salsa tartufata and RucolaCress	74
Mangetout, truffle honey and fresh Belgian goat cheese	77
Chocolate brownie with truffle honey	79

SUMMER

Roasted leek tagliatelle with marjoram, turnips and argan oil 83
Open lasagne with watermelon, fennel carpaccio, dill, baby spinach, yellow cherry tomatoes and lemon 85
Cold watercress soup with Hippo Tops, redcurrants and argan oil 89
Yellow carrot and chervil salad with nori, sesame and ice tea 90
Sweet pepper caviar with marjoram, green olives, burrata flakes and Aclla Cress 92
Cucumber lasagne with raspberry, lemon verbena, lemon juice and Iluigi's olive ice cream 95
Apricot marmalade with lavender, fresh yogurt, olive oil and Limon Cress 99
Spaghetti with yellow courgette, baby spinach and wild garlic, Motti Cress and toasted bread topping 100
Pattypan squash burgers with mozzarella, roasted leek and fresh thyme 104
Cucumber salad with Thai basil, shallot, lime, red chilli, roasted peanuts and Syrha Leaves 107
Fresh cherries with cottage cheese, fresh lemon balm, honey and apple blossoms 111
Bitter chocolate chunks with olive oil, coarse sea salt and Limon Cress 112
Braised spring onion with lemon verbena, paprika and flax seeds 115

AUTUMN

Fork-crushed potatoes and chestnut mushroom carpaccio with Motti Cress and celery sauce 121
Chard spaghetti with shiitake, cashew nuts and Citra Leaves 125
Kohlrabi ravioli and purple cauliflower with hazelnuts and Jasmine Blossoms 126
Braised carrot with ginger, green asparagus, lime and sunflower seeds 130
Roasted onion stew with chestnut mushroom, savory and grated radish 135
Rigatoni with broccoli pesto, lemon, roasted red onion, fresh apricots and Jasmine Blossoms 139
Crushed strawberry with ginger, courgette, pistachio ice cream and Limon Cress 140
Radish vermicelli with fresh goat cheese, roasted buckwheat, Légumaise Italia and Adji Cress 144
Salad of green grapes and sweet potato, black sesame, dill, lime, yellow cherry tomato and Anise Blossoms 147
Braised celery sticks with creamy potatoes, goat cheese and caviar 149
Shallot with turmeric, cauliflower and cucumber with curry 152

WINTER

Celeriac grilled over an open fire with gomasio, rosemary, vinaigrette of pink grapefruit, cranberries and Ghoa Cress 159

White cabbage tagliatelle, mashed red cabbage, hazelnut, pumpernickel bread crusts and Lupine Cress 161

Turnip royal with Kyona Mustard Cress 164

Sweet potato hummus with sesame crackers and Cuzco Leaves 170

Roasted chickpea chermoula with briefly braised endive, lemon and Gangnam Tops 173

Chicory poached in orange, pine cone, liquorice, fresh tarragon and clove broth 175

Roasted winter carrots with cumin, radish sprouts and Hippo Tops 176

Red chicory salad and fried orange slices with mixed spice and Shiso Green 178

Brussels sprouts skewer on the BBQ with apple-elderberry compote and Scarlet Cress 181

Baked potato with raw Jerusalem artichoke strands, argan oil, caviar and Persinette Cress 185

Pumpkin blinis with fresh cheese and Maoi Caviar 188

Grilled winter leek with beetroot-pear coulis, puffed black rice and Scarlet Cress 193

Pear compote with ginger and turmeric, nocciola olive ice cream, roasted hazelnut and Yka Leaves 195

Open pumpkin ravioli with Achelse blue crumble, parsley sauce and Yka Leaves 196

Yellow beetroot rolls with shiitake-hazelnut filling, Légumaise truffle and RucolaCress 198

WEIGHTS FOR DRY INGREDIENTS

20 g	¾ oz
40 g	1½ oz
50 g	2 oz
60 g	2½ oz
100 g	3½ oz
125 g	4 oz
150 g	5 oz
200 g	7 oz
250 g	9 oz
400 g	14 oz
500 g	1 lb 2 oz
800 g	1¾ lb
1 kg	2¼ lb

LIQUID MEASURES

METRIC	IMPERIAL US
50 ml	2 fl oz ¼ cup
250 ml	8 fl oz 1 cup
1 litre	1¾ pints 1 quart

OVEN TEMPERATURES

°C	°F
100	212
120	250
140	275
180	350

WHO ARE 'WE'?

Ilse and **Frank** have been a strong team for several years now. Their culinary television program called *Z-Mastercooks* on Kanaal Z is currently one of the most-watched programmes on the platform, and Ilse is also the regular host and presenter in Frank's project We're Smart® World. In their newest programme on Kanaal Z, *De Keukentafel* ('The Kitchen Table'), they join forces to look out for sustainable initiatives.

The combination of Ilse's passion to design ceramics and Frank's belief that we should be creative with vegetables, formed the solid foundation and was a small step towards creating a surprising 'wild' cookbook together!

We're Smart® World is the undisputed go-to reference in the culinary world of vegetables and is the brainchild of **Frank Fol, The Vegetables Chef®**.

Every year the We're Smart® Green Guide recognizes the best vegetable restaurants in the world with 1 to 5 radishes, and vegetable chefs and companies with the We're Smart® Best Vegetables Restaurants Awards and We're Smart® Future Awards. In this way We're Smart® World contributes to a healthy, sustainable and ecological world.

www.weresmartworld.com

Ilse De Vis from WILD MOON creates artisanal, handmade ceramics.
Making the ultimate cup, plate or bowl is something that gives her joy.

In contrast to her daily life, where she is a presenter on the television chain Kanaal Z and at major events, ceramics is something that brings her closer to herself.
Each piece is unique and hand made. *With love, for life.*

Wild Cooking with images that leave you wanting more.

For the photography for Wild Cooking, we were honoured to work together with internationally renowned photographer **Wim Demessemaekers,** also known as **the Soul Food Photographer.** Wim is not just an exceptional photographer; he is a storyteller through and through. His photography creates stories that inspire and bring dreams to life — from the magic on our plate to his other passion, wildlife photography. Wim strives to create pure and authentic images. He chooses to work with vintage lenses, essential guides in his search for illuminating perspectives.

Wim is devoted to inspiring and generating impact. And that goes beyond photography. As one of the driving forces behind **Soul Food Revolution**, he creates maximum impact for initiatives around healthy and sustainable food. Soul Food Revolution is a purpose-driven creative agency that embodies the essence of communication: moving and inspiring people with a strong and authentic story by creating strong brands, inspiring campaigns, and mouth-watering websites…

From passionate farmers to chefs who can conjure up a veritable revolution on your plate. From game-changing producers to retailers who aren't afraid to make bold choices. Wim is there to help anyone involved with sustainable food to make a real difference — for themselves and for the planet.

Food is life.

SPRING

SPRING

THE HEALTHY BREAKFAST!

4 SERVINGS

 30 MINUTES    VEGGIES    FRUITS   ☾ LARGE FLAT PLATES (WILD MOON)

Stir-fried cauliflower and turnip greens with Greek yogurt and oatmeal

Watermelon-lime drink with mint

Ripe blueberries

Crackers with carrot salad and Kikuna Leaves

Fresh water with celery and Motti Cress

Watermelon 'fingers'

STIR-FRIED CAULIFLOWER AND TURNIP GREENS WITH GREEK YOGURT AND OATMEAL

RECIPE

Remove the greens and then wash and cut the cauliflower into slices.
Coarsely chop turnip greens into equal pieces.
Stir-fry both with some olive oil and season with sea salt.
Divide between the 4 bowls and spoon some yogurt on top.
Finish with the oatmeal.
Serve lukewarm or cold.

INGREDIENTS

1 small cauliflower
1 turnip
tablespoon of olive oil (Iluigi)
freshly ground sea salt (Verstegen)
160 g Greek yogurt
4 teaspoons of oatmeal (without sugar)

WATERMELON-LIME DRINK WITH MINT

RECIPE

Peel the watermelon and cut into pieces.
Place in a blender and add the lime juice and a few mint leaves.
Mix into a drink.
Put juice in the glasses and finish with a sprig of mint.

INGREDIENTS

1 small ripe watermelon (seedless)
juice of 2 limes
a few sprigs of fresh mint

CRACKERS WITH CARROT SALAD AND KIKUNA LEAVES

RECIPE

Mix everything and make 2 sandwiches per person with the crackers and carrot salad mixture.
Place in each bowl with some Kikuna leaves.

INGREDIENTS

200 g grated carrots

150 g organic Légumaise Brabant, carrot with ginger

sprig of curly parsley, finely chopped

1 shallot, finely chopped

freshly ground black pepper (Verstegen)

1 cup of Kikuna Leaves (Koppert Cress)

16 crackers of your choice

FRESH WATER WITH CELERY AND MOTTI CRESS

RECIPE

Pour water (still or sparkling) into glass. Place a stick of celery and some Motti Cress in it. Allow to infuse for a while.

INGREDIENTS

4 celery sticks

1 cup of Motti Cress (Koppert Cress)

still or sparkling water

BREAKFAST CAN ALSO BE DELICIOUSLY TRENDY!

Lack of time, bad habits and loneliness at the breakfast table are major culprits when it comes to skipping the most important meal of the day. As the first meal, breakfast should contain the necessary energy and vitamins to start a busy day. The fact very few people eat breakfast is already a problem in itself. Throughout the workweek, breakfast mainly has a negative connotation; parents are nervous, the bus or the car is waiting up front to leave, and so on. Habits related to eating or making time for breakfast mainly have to do with existing family traditions, but also with what's important to parents or an individual's character. Eating a healthy breakfast is an even more difficult step …

The organization of a successful breakfast starts the day before.
- What do I want to do myself a favour with tomorrow morning?
- Why should I definitely wake up on time tomorrow?

Two questions that everyone should ask from time to time. Good organization ensures that all ingredients for the ultimate breakfast are present. If this is the case, you can already prepare a few things before going to bed, in order to save time and gain quality. Eating healthily also means eating calmly. Social contact usually makes this moment a bit cosier too. If better organization can give us this quality time, then it's already an important step in the right direction! This is what we like to do during weekends or holidays, right?

How can we make breakfast healthier? Variety is the magic word here. But really alternate — not a day of chocolate and a piece of chocolate the day after. Breakfast starts with good, wholemeal bread or cereals. But we must also dare to experiment at breakfast. Vegetables can play an important role here. For example, vegetable and fruit juices in combination with cold milk. Raw vegetables cut into sticks can also taste nice and fresh. A piece of ripe fruit or a fruit salad can certainly taste great on a regular basis. Even more creative are the fruit and vegetable marmalades with little or no added sugars mixed with a pot of low-fat yogurt.

NUTRISCORE **A**

SPRING

GRILLED TOAST WITH APPLE-TOMATO MARMALADE, TRUFFLE DUST AND FLOREGANO

4 SERVINGS

 25 MINUTES  VEGGIES  FRUIT  LARGE FLAT PLATE (WILD MOON)

RECIPE

Marmelade:
Peel and core the apples. Cut into pieces.
Wash tomatoes and remove the tough central core.
Make a cross cut at the top of the tomatoes.
Bring enough water to the boil and immerse the tomatoes for 20 sec to loosen the skin. Then take them out and plunge them into cold water and then peel. Now cut the tomatoes into quarters and remove the seeds.
Put the seeds into a blender or food processor and blend to a pulp, then sieve the pulp and add it to the peeled tomatoes.
Season with a pinch of mace powder.
Stew the apples and tomatoes covered, over low heat until it forms a thick marmalade. This can take up to 30 minutes.

Toast:
Using a bread knife, cut slices 1.5 to 2 cm thick.
Grill these on the (Berghoff) BBQ until they are nicely toasted on both sides. Then spoon the marmalade onto the toast.
This can be served hot or cold.

Serve:
Put 2 pieces of toast on each plate and garnish with some truffle dust and the Floregano.

INGREDIENTS

2 stewing apples
4 ripe beef tomatoes
a pinch of mace powder (Verstegen)
truffle powder
1 small loaf wholemeal bread
1 cup of Floregano (Koppert Cress)

TECHNIQUES: MARMALADE, GRILL, RAW, STEW   **SUGGESTED BEVERAGE:** MARY V, TOMATO JUICE (NICK BRIL)

SPRING

CUCUMBER GAZPACHO WITH KEFIR AND MELISSA CRESS

4 SERVINGS

 20 MINUTES    VEGGIES    SMALL BOWL (WILD MOON)

RECIPE

Gazpacho:
Cut the cucumber.
Peel the onion and garlic and chop finely.
Put everything in a bowl and moisten with white wine vinegar and olive oil.
Season with sea salt, cayenne pepper and cumin powder.
Marinate a little.
Then mix with a blender or food processor until an emulsion forms.
Add a little water if necessary. Place in refrigerator for storage.

Serve:
Divide the gazpacho evenly over the bowls, spoon in kefir to taste (up to half). Finish with the cress.

INGREDIENTS

1 cucumber

1 onion

1 clove of garlic

generous dash of white wine vinegar

generous splash of olive oil (Iluigi)

freshly ground sea salt (Verstegen)

ground cayenne pepper (Verstegen)

pinch of cumin powder (Verstegen)

500 g of kefir

1 cup of Melissa Cress (Koppert Cress)

TECHNIQUES:
RAW, SOUP, EMULSION

SPRING

SMAAKBOM® SALSA WITH LÉGUMAISE THAI AND GHOA CRESS

4 SERVINGS

 20 MINUTES    VEGGIES    SMALL BOWL (WILD MOON)

RECIPE

Salad Mix:
Cut the bell pepper, fennel, radish and mango into medium dice. Finely chop the fresh coriander.
Toss everything with the olive oil, sea salt, lime juice and ginger.

Serve:
Divide the mix over the 4 bowls. Spoon the Légumaise on top. Finish with the cress.

WHAT'S A *SMAAKBOM*®?

Smaakbom®, or Flavor Bomb, is a protected trademark of We're Smart® World, by Frank Fol. It stands for the flavorFOL creations that have been developed according to the Think Vegetables! Think Fruit!® philosophy and which boast the following advantages:
- tasty, healthy & full of character
- regionally seasonal
- fruits & vegetables predominate, minimum 80%
- natural colours
- without added flavour enhancers, sugars or preservatives
- always with Légumaise®, the healthy sauce
- your daily vegetable flavour portion!

A *Smaakbom*® can be a snack, a side dish or a full meal.
Enjoy healthily while you can!

INGREDIENTS

150 g red bell pepper
150 g fennel
150 g radishes
150 g ripe mango
20 g fresh coriander
generous dash of olive oil (Iluigi)
freshly ground sea salt (Verstegen)
juice of 1/2 lime
10 g finely chopped fresh ginger
150 g Bio Légumaise Thai, red curry with coconut
1 cup of Ghoa Cress (Koppert Cress)

TECHNIQUES: RAW, SAUCE, EMULSION   **SUGGESTED BEVERAGE:** MARY V, TOMATO JUICE (NICK BRIL)

NUTRISCORE **A**

SPRING

BBQ CROQUE RADISH WITH MUSHROOM AND TRUFFLE LÉGUMAISE AND GARDEN CRESS

4 SERVINGS

 20 MINUTES    VEGGIES    LARGE FLAT PLATE (WILD MOON)

RECIPE

Smoked onion:
Peel and cut the onion, and smoke it briefly.
To smoke the onion we use some oak wood flakes.
Put these in a frying pan, place an inverted deep plate over it and put a grill over that.
Spread the onion on this grill and heat the pan.
As soon as the wood starts to smoulder, put the lid on the pan and wait until the pan is full of smoke.
Then set the pan aside and let the onions absorb the smoke for another 5 to 10 minutes. Then they can be removed from the 'smoke oven'.

Croque:
Cut 8 slices of bread no more than 1.5 cm thick with a bread knife.
Spread some Légumaise on 4 of the slices.
Cut the leaves off the radishes and wash the radishes and leaves.
Slice the radishes and then spread the radish slices on the 4 pieces of bread topped with sauce.
Place some radish greens on top, then put the smoked onion and some spinach leaves on top.
Finally, crumble some cheese over each croque and close with the second slice of bread and press firmly.
Grill these on the (Berghoff) BBQ until they are nicely toasted and warm on both sides.

Serve:
Place a croque cut in half on each plate, garnish with some truffle Légumaise, some extra chunks of cheese, some white truffle sea salt, a few drops of olive oil and the cress.

INGREDIENTS

150 g Bio Légumaise Périgord, mushroom with truffle

1 bunch large radishes with greens

1 large red onion

40 g young spinach

120 g 'Flandrien Oud' (crumbled cheese)

generous dash of olive oil (Iluigi)

white truffle sea salt

1 cup of Garden Cress (Koppert Cress)

1 small wholemeal bread (not pre-cut)

TECHNIQUES: GRILL, RAW, EMULSION, SMOKE

SUGGESTED BEVERAGE: PURE RED (WINE CASTLE VANDEURZEN, BELGIUM)

HOW DO YOU KNOW YOU'RE ON THE RIGHT TRACK?

Measuring is knowing... Wild Cooking not only wants to inspire you, we also want to help you make the right choices. That's why you will also find a NutriScore for every dish, from A to E. This scoring system helps consumers make healthier choices when cooking. NutriScore is a 5-level, colour-coded nutrition rating system, where A (green) is the preferred choice and E (red) is a not the optimal choice as part of your regular diet. But sometimes you can also really enjoy some variety, for example, by trying our chocolate recipe (which is rated E). To help you make the best choices, the NutriScore for each recipe has been calculated for you.

VEGETABLE AND FRUIT OF THE YEAR!

Each year, for over ten years, We're Smart® World focuses on a fruit and vegetable during the Week of Fruit and Vegetables. This annual week in May is a momentum on which all stakeholders communicate or launch new initiatives. In 2021, we drew worldwide attention to paprika and watermelon. We are all familiar with these tasty and natural ingredients. Paprika has been used frequently in vegetable mixes, raw or stirred, and in the oven or on the grill it is a true treat. Watermelon on the other hand refreshes on hot summer days. You can find it in a sweet fruit salad, but it tastes great as well combined with vegetables.

SPRING

PEA SOUP WITH LEMON BALM, FRIED SHALLOTS, SWEET POTATO AND SEA FENNEL

4 SERVINGS

 30 MINUTES  VEGGIES  LARGE FLAT PLATE (WILD MOON)

RECIPE

Sweet potato:
Peel the sweet potato, cut into quarters and cook in water with sea salt.

Fried shallot:
Heat the fryer to 140 °C.
Peel the shallots and slice in very thin rings and make sure they are dry by drying them with kitchen paper.
Toss the shallot rings in the flour and fry until crispy and lightly browned.
Place the fried shallots on kitchen paper and shake them a bit so that most of the fat is absorbed. Season with a pinch of smoked sea salt.

Soup:
Peel the onion and garlic and chop finely.
Wash leeks and chop finely.
Stew these in some olive oil.
Moisten with water and season with smoked sea salt and black pepper.
Now add the peas and some finely chopped lemon balm leaves and cook gently for 5 minutes before blending.

Serve:
Ladle the soup (hot or cold) into the bowls, place some pieces of sweet potato and fried shallot over the soup and garnish with a few sprigs of sea fennel.

INGREDIENTS

1 sweet potato
2 shallots
1 tablespoon of flour
1 onion
2 cloves of garlic
1 leek
some olive oil (Iluigi)
smoked sea salt (Verstegen)
freshly ground black pepper (Verstegen)
400 g peas (may be frozen)
2 branches of lemon balm
sea fennel (Koppert Cress)
water

TECHNIQUES: SOUP, RAW, FRY, COOK

SUGGESTED BEVERAGE: PINOT NOIR PURE RED (WINE CASTLE VANDEURZEN, BELGIUM)

SPRING

FINGER FOOD: SHISO LEAVES GREEN WITH A CELERY, TOMATO, EGG MIMOSA AND WHITE TRUFFLE OIL SPREAD

4 SERVINGS

 30 MINUTES  VEGGIES  LARGE FLAT PLATE (WILD MOON)

RECIPE

Spread:
Peel the boiled eggs and crush them with a fork.
Wash the celery and cut the stalk into small dice.
Mix everything with the Légumaise and add a few drops of white truffle oil, some sea salt and black pepper.
Mix everything into a spread.

Serve:
Take a Shiso leaf and top with a spoonful of spread.
Fold and eat with your fingers.

INGREDIENTS

1 stick of white celery

4 hard-boiled eggs

1 tray of Shiso Leaves Green (Koppert Cress)

150 g Bio Légumaise Italia, tomato with basil

white truffle oil

freshly ground sea salt (Verstegen)

freshly ground black pepper (Verstegen)

TECHNIQUES: RAW, COOK, EMULSION, SAUCE, MARINATE

SUGGESTED BEVERAGE: ROSÉ PINOT MEUNIER (WINE CASTLE VANDEURZEN, BELGIUM)

SPRING

BBQ SHALLOT "OYSTERS" WITH POTATO, RASPBERRY AND LIMON CRESS

4 SERVINGS

 60 MINUTES  VEGGIES  FRUITS  SERVING BOWL (WILD MOON)

RECIPE

Sour shallots:
Peel 2 shallots and cut into fine rings.
Season with sea salt and black pepper and marinate in raspberry vinegar while the remaining shallots are cooking.

BBQ:
Place 10 unpeeled shallots on a gently smouldering BBQ so they don't burn. Turn once in a while.
This can take up to 30 minutes.
When cooked, the outer layer will be black and you will see blisters on the outside of the shallot.
Let them rest for a while, away from the fire, then cut them in half lengthwise and separate the cooked shallot from the burnt skin.
We are now going to fill each half shallot.

Mashed potatoes:
Wash and cut the potatoes into large pieces, then boil them in salted water.
Once tender, drain but leave some of the cooking water in the bottom of the pot and then mash.
Now add a few drops of argan oil, the raspberry vinegar
(from the marinade for the sour shallots) and all of the raspberries (except 10 beautiful raspberries that we keep for garnish).
Mix everything well, add some additional seasoning if necessary.
Now fill the shallot "oysters" with a spoonful of raspberry-potato puree and top with half a raspberry and some slightly sour shallot.

Serve:
Place 5 "oysters" on each plate and garnish with some Limon Cress.
Serve warm, cold or lukewarm.

TECHNIQUES: RAW, COOK, SOUR, GRILL

SUGGESTED BEVERAGE: GRÜNER VELTLINER PRESTIGE, PURE WHITE (WINE CASTLE VANDEURZEN, BELGIUM)

INGREDIENTS

12 long shallots
sea salt (Verstegen)
freshly ground black pepper (Verstegen)
dash of raspberry vinegar
200 g gently boiled potatoes (peeled)
drops of argan oil (Arqan)
100 g fresh raspberries
1 cup of Limon Cress (Koppert Cress)

SPRING

CHARD-PEACH PILLOWS WITH GRILLED CHARD STICKS, CHERMOULA AND VENE CRESS

4 SERVINGS

 45 MINUTES  VEGGIES  FRUITS  LARGE FLAT PLATE (WILD MOON)

RECIPE

Pillows:

Separate chard leaves from stalks and wash both.
Blanch 12 leaves in boiling salted water for 1 minute and then place in ice water.
Cut 12 equal pieces from the stalks (about 10 cm each) and season them with olive oil, sea salt and chermoula powder.
Mix well and let it marinate for a while.
Finely chop the remaining leaves and stalks and braise them in some olive oil with sea salt and black pepper.

Peel, cut and wash the potatoes and the onion. Bring to the boil with some sea salt and cook until tender. Drain almost all of the liquid. Then mash the potatoes with some of the cooking liquid using a pestle or fork. Wash and pit the peach, then cut into pieces and mix with the mashed potatoes.
Stir in the braised Swiss chard, a good dash of olive oil and some black pepper. Mix well.

Now fill each leaf with a firm scoop of chard-peach-potato mixture and fold closed. (If the leaves are too big, cut a little first.) Do this 12 times to make 3 "pillows" per person.
Then rub each pillow with olive oil. The chard stems can now be placed on the hot BBQ. Grill well on both sides.
They should be lightly charred and retain some structure.

Serve:

Place the cushions on the BBQ to heat them up (or in an oven) and place 3 on each plate.
Place a piece of warm stem on top of each cushion.
Garnish with some extra chermoula powder and Vene Cress leaves.

INGREDIENTS

1 Swiss chard stalk and leaves (chard)

olive oil (Iluigi)

freshly ground sea salt (Verstegen)

chermoula powder (Verstegen)

freshly ground black pepper (Verstegen)

400 g soft boiling potato

1 onion

2 ripe peaches

1 cup of Vene Cress (Koppert Cress)

TECHNIQUES: GRILL, BRAISE, COOK, RAW, MASHED POTATOES, POTATO STEW

SUGGESTED BEVERAGE: DELVAUX BEER (BREWERY DE KROON, BELGIUM)

HERBS AND SPICES, A WORLD OF DIFFERENCE!

Professional chefs and hobby chefs agree: herbs should always be in every kitchen. Each type of herb provides a unique aromatic experience on your plate. And what's equally important: they stimulate your appetite and digestion. Once a chef has mastered the secrets of herbs and spices, it opens up a new world. But be careful, dosing correctly is key, such as combining the right flavors. For *Wild Cooking* we have elaborated multiple beautiful combinations in taste with the herbs and spices of **Verstegen**. We wish you lots of cooking pleasure trying them all out.

NUTRISCORE **A**

SPRING

CABBAGE WUSHI WITH QUINOA, MITSUNA LETTUCE, THAI BASIL, BLACK SESAME AND LÉGUMAISE THAI

4 SERVINGS

 30 MINUTES (+ RESTING TIME IN THE FRIDGE)  VEGGIES  FLAT PLATE (WILD MOON)

RECIPE

Cook the quinoa as stated on the packaging. Allow to cool.
Finely chop the basil leaves.
Mix cold quinoa with basil, Légumaise, a few drops of argan oil, some finely chopped mitsuna, sea salt and black sesame seeds.

Wushi rolls:

Take 4 large outer leaves from the pointed cabbage.
Wash them carefully to avoid tearing.
Steam or boil them until smooth. Cool in ice water.
Cut the central ribs away from the leaf.
Finely chop the ribs and stir into the quinoa mix.
Now cut a piece of cling film for each roll.
Dry each leaf and place on a piece of cling film with the largest side up.
Cover each leaf with slightly larger mitsuna leaves.
Now spoon the quinoa mix onto each cabbage leaf like a sausage or like a wrap.
Roll up firmly from bottom to top and now roll the foil so that you can tighten it on both sides by rolling it up.
Place on a plate in the refrigerator for at least one hour.

Serve:

Now use a sharp knife to cut 5 to 6 rolls of about 3 cm high for each plate, like a sushi roll.
Remove the cling film and arrange the wushi in a circle on each plate.
Spoon some Légumaise in the middle and garnish with a few mitsuna leaves and a few extra drops of argan oil.

INGREDIENTS

200 g quinoa

2 branches of fresh Thai basil

150 g Légumaise Thai, red curry with coconut

argan oil (Arqan)

100 g mitsuna lettuce

freshly ground sea salt (Verstegen)

2 teaspoons of black sesame seeds (Verstegen)

1 small pointed cabbage

TECHNIQUES: STEAMING, COOKING, RAW, EMULSION

SUGGESTED BEVERAGE: CHARDONNAY PURE WHITE (WINE CASTLE VANDEURZEN, BELGIUM)

SPRING

ASPARAGUS SPAGHETTI WITH POTATO STRAWS, CAVIAR AND RUCOLACRESS

4 SERVINGS

 25 MINUTES    VEGGIES    DEEP PLATE (WILD MOON)

RECIPE

Potato straws:
Cut the potato into thin slices with a mandoline or vegetable peeler. Then cut the slices into fine threads with a knife. Wash under running water and dry.
Fry the potato threads at 140 °C until they are crispy and have turned a beautiful golden yellow.
Place on kitchen paper and sprinkle with a bit of sea salt.

Asparagus spaghetti:
Peel 8 asparagus spears. Cut them into thin slices (2 mm) using a vegetable peeler.
Now cut long strings (spaghetti).
Braise the strings briefly with a dash of water and 20 g butter.
Season with sea salt and black pepper.
Make sure they are still al dente.

Asparagus sauce:
Peel the 4 remaining asparagus.
Cut into pieces and cook with a little water.
Season with sea salt, some mace and some black pepper.
Mix this with the cooking liquid and the remaining butter to make a thickened white sauce.

Serve:
Spoon some sauce into each bowl.
Using a fork, roll some asparagus spaghetti into a nest and place on each one of the plates.
Garnish with some crispy potato straws, a spoonful of caviar and some RucolaCress.

INGREDIENTS

1 gently boiled potato (peeled)
sea salt (Verstegen)
12 thick spears of white asparagus
60 g butter
freshly ground black pepper (Verstegen)
mace powder (Verstegen)
160 g caviar
1 cup of RucolaCress (Koppert Cress)

TECHNIQUES: RAW, COOK, STEW, SAUCE, FRY

SUGGESTED BEVERAGE: CHARDONNAY CARAT PURE WHITE (WINE CASTLE VANDEURZEN, BELGIUM)

NUTRISCORE **A**

SPRING

BBQ POINTED CABBAGE STEAK WITH RADISH SAUCE, CASHEW NUTS, ARGAN OIL AND KYONA MUSTARD CRESS

4 SERVINGS

 25 MINUTES  VEGGIES   NUTS  LARGE DEEP PLATE (WILD MOON)

RECIPE

Radish sauce:
Use 2/3 of the radishes without greens.
Wash briefly and cut in half.
Bring to the boil with some water and a little smoked salt.
When the radishes are tender, remove them from the cooking water and mix them with a dash of olive oil to make a nice pink sauce.

Pointed cabbage:
Wash the pointed cabbage and cut it into quarters.
Brush each wedge with olive oil, season with smoked sea salt, black pepper and a little mace.
Place these over a low fire on the BBQ and grill the cabbage until browned on both sides.
Then roast them together on a tray for another 10 minutes in an oven preheated to 180 °C.
Cut the remaining radishes into sticks.

Serve:
Place a warm piece of pointed cabbage on each plate.
Spoon some radish sauce next to the grilled cabbage and garnish with the radish sticks, a radish leaf, the cashew nuts, a few drops of argan oil and some Kyona Mustard Cress.

INGREDIENTS

1 bunch radishes
smoked sea salt (Verstegen)
1 pointed cabbage
olive oil (Iluigi)
freshly ground black pepper (Verstegen)
mace powder (Verstegen)
50 g chopped cashew nuts
argan oil (Arqan)
1 cup of Kyona Mustard Cress (Koppert Cress)

TECHNIQUES: GRILL, ROAST, RAW, COOK, STEW, SAUCE
SUGGESTED BEVERAGE: SUPER KROON BEER (BREWERY DE KROON, BELGIUM)

A KNIFE HAS TO CUT!

Do you sometimes curse when the knife doesn't cut well enough? That's why it's important to purchase a good quality knife from the start. If you take care of a good knife with respect, you can use it for a lifetime.

A few tips:
- Always wash a knife by hand under running water. Avoid the dishwasher.
- Always store a knife safely; a special drawer, a knife block, a knife magnet or a knife protector are all good choices.
- It is important to keep a knife sharp. So, sharpen it regularly. A good knife does not require much force to cut.
- Always choose the right knife to cut the right product. Not only will it be easier, but it will also be safer!

Looking for good knives? We always use **BergHOFF** to do some wild cooking!

SPRING

BRAISED TURNIPS WITH REDCURRANT, TEMPRANILLO, GOMASIO AND MUSTARD CRESS

4 SERVINGS

 30 MINUTES    VEGGIES    FRUITS    MEDIUM DEEP PLATE (WILD MOON)

RECIPE

Turnips:
Cut the green tops off of each turnip about 3 cm above the turnip.
Next, peel 10 turnips and cut them in half so that each piece also has some green.
Take a stew pot, add a dash of olive oil and place the turnips next to each other.
Moisten with some water and season with sea salt.
Braise under a lid until the water has completely evaporated.
Now season with some gomasio and then fry lightly on both sides until nicely browned.

Sauce:
Take 4 more turnips and peel them. Cut into pieces.
Place in a stew pot with a dash of olive oil, half of the redcurrants and pour in the red wine until submerged.
Season with some sea salt and black pepper.
Stew covered over low heat.
When the turnips are tender, use a blender to blend it into a smooth sauce (add extra wine if needed).

Serve:
Place the warm sauce in the centre of each plate, put 5 turnip halves on each plate and garnish with a few drops of olive oil, some redcurrants and the cress.

INGREDIENTS

2 bunches of small spring turnips

olive oil (Iluigi)

freshly ground sea salt (Verstegen)

gomasio mix (Verstegen)

1 small bowl of redcurrants

generous dash of red Tempranillo wine

freshly ground black pepper (Verstegen)

1 cup of Mustard Cress (Koppert Cress)

TECHNIQUES: BRAISE, STEW, SAUCE, RAW, BAKE

SUGGESTED BEVERAGE: TEMPRANILLO PRESTIGE PURE RED (WINE CASTLE VANDEURZEN, BELGIUM)

NUTRISCORE A

SPRING

RIPE PEAR AND FENNEL CARPACCIO, PINK GRAPEFRUIT, PISTACHIO, GOJI BERRY AND YKA LEAVES

4 SERVINGS

 15 MINUTES  VEGGIES  FRUITS  LARGE FLAT PLATE (WILD MOON)

RECIPE

Marinade:
Cut the fennel into very thin slices with a mandoline.
Season with sea salt and black pepper.
Squeeze the grapefruit and add the juice to the fennel.
Now add some olive oil as well.
Mix everything well and let it marinate briefly.

Carpaccio:
Peel and core the pears.
Slice thinly and make a circle with the slices on each plate.
Spread the marinated fennel evenly on top.
Spoon the juice over it.

Serve:
Finely chop the Yka Leaves and sprinkle over the fennel.
Garnish with the pistachio nuts and the goji berries.

INGREDIENTS

1 fennel bulb
coarse sea salt (Verstegen)
freshly ground black pepper (Verstegen)
1 pink grapefruit
2 ripe pears of your choice
1 cup of Yka Leaves (Koppert Cress)
40 g pistachio nuts peeled and chopped
40 g goji berries

TECHNIQUES: RAW, MARINATE **SUGGESTED BEVERAGE:** ALBARIÑO PURE WHITE (WINE CASTLE VANDEURZEN, BELGIUM)

HOW DO OLIVE VARIETIES DETERMINE THE TASTE OF OIL?

An olive tree gives optimal results after 15 years. And, for 1 litre of extra virgin olive oil, between 5 to 8 kilos of olives are needed, depending on the quality. Iluigi olive oil uses 8 kilos, to guarantee optimal quality. The acidity of the 'juice' is decisive in this, as this may be a maximum of 0.8. As grape varieties are important to the flavour of a wine, in addition to the soil and the climate, the choice of olive varieties also determines the taste of the olive oil!
There are different olive varieties, but a few of them are commonly used to make high-quality olive oil:

- Arbequina: green apple, mango, grassy, balanced
- Hojiblanca: tomato, arugula, spicy
- Picudo: buttery, nutty, bitter touch
- Ocal: velvety and mild
- Cornicabra: outspoken citrus, with green plant-based taste
- Moraiolo: nicely balanced, aromatic and very fruity in the nose
- Canino: slightly fruity, spicy and beautifully green
- Frantoio: very fruity, green and rounded taste

For their organic, extra-virgin olive oil, **Iluigi** primarily uses the Canino & Frantoio olive varieties, which are cultivated in the beautiful Italian olive groves around Bolsena. The result is a greenish, mildly fruity and spicy olive oil with a very low acidity that tastes heavenly on our culinary creations. Thank you, nature!

SPRING

GRILLED HONEY-LACQUERED RHUBARB, GINGER NUT CRUMBLE, OLIVE ICE CREAM AND HONNY CRESS

4 SERVINGS

25 MINUTES · FRUITS · SMALL BOWL + COFFEE CUP (WILD MOON)

RECIPE

Rhubarb:
Wash and peel the rhubarb and cut into 12 equal pieces of about 8 cm. Coat them with the honey using a brush.
Grill them over a low heat on the BBQ until they are almost tender. Place 3 pieces on each plate.

Serve:
Serve lukewarm or cold. Place a scoop of olive ice cream on each plate and crumble the ginger nut biscuits over it. Garnish with the Honny Cress.

INGREDIENTS

2 rhubarb stalks

2 tablespoons of honey of your choice

4 scoops of olive ice cream (Iluigi)

2 ginger nut biscuits

1 cup of Honny Cress (Koppert Cress)

TECHNIQUES:
GRILL, RAW, MARINATE

SUGGESTED BEVERAGE:
CUP OF COFFEE

SPRING

STRAWBERRY-RHUBARB SWEET WITH LEMON AND PAZTIZZ TOPS

4 SERVINGS

 15 MINUTES    FRUITS    SMALL BOWL (WILD MOON)

RECIPE

Rhubarb:
Peel the rhubarb and cut it into wafer-thin slices (10 cm) with the help of a vegetable peeler. Place them in a bowl and add the lemon juice. Leave to marinate for a few minutes.

Sweets:
Wash and hull the strawberries.
Roll each strawberry in a slice of rhubarb. If necessary, pierce with a cocktail stick to keep everything together.
The sweet strawberry provides a nice counterbalance to the fresh sourness of the rhubarb.

Serve:
Place the sweets in the bowls and finish with a few drops of argan oil and a sprig of Paztizz Tops on each sweet.
Fantastic for hot days and with a glass of delicious rosé.

INGREDIENTS

2 rhubarb stalks
juice of 1 lemon
250 to 500 g of ripe strawberries
drops of argan oil (Arqan)
1 cup of Paztizz Tops (Koppert Cress)

TECHNIQUES: RAW, MARINATE   **SUGGESTED BEVERAGE:** ROSÉ PINOT MEUNIER (WINE CASTLE VANDEURZEN, BELGIUM)

SPRING

CAULIFLOWER SLICES
WITH CREMA DI TARTUFI BIANCHI & PERSINETTE
+
RAW ASPARAGUS CURLS
WITH SALSA TARTUFATA AND RUCOLACRESS

4 SERVINGS

 15 MINUTES  VEGGIES  LARGE FLAT PLATE (WILD MOON)

RECIPE

Cauliflower:
Wash and cut the cauliflower into slices of about 4 mm.
Spoon a little crema on each slice of cauliflower and top with a few sprigs of Persinette Cress.

Asparagus:
Peel the asparagus.
Use a vegetable peeler to cut fine slices or strips of asparagus. Be gentle and make a loose knot with each strip without over-tightening it so that it does not tear.
Spoon a little tartufata on each curl and top with a few sprigs of Arugula Cress.

Serve:
Make as many as you want and place on a plate.

INGREDIENTS

1 piece of cauliflower

1 jar of crema di tartufi bianchi

1 cup of Persinette (Koppert Cress)

4 thick spears of white asparagus

1 jar of salsa tartufata

1 cup of RucolaCress (Koppert Cress)

TECHNIQUES: RAW, SAUCE
SUGGESTED BEVERAGE: CHARDONNAY PRESTIGE PURE WHITE (WINE CASTLE VANDEURZEN, BELGIUM)

SPRING

MANGETOUT, TRUFFLE HONEY AND FRESH BELGIAN GOAT CHEESE

4 SERVINGS

 10 MINUTES    VEGGIES    SMALL ROUND PLATE (WILD MOON)

RECIPE

Cut mangetout lengthwise into narrow strips.
Place a piece of goat cheese on each plate and put some of the mangetout next to it.

Serve:
Finish with a spoonful of truffle honey on the cheese and radish sprouts.

INGREDIENTS

80 g mangetout
120 g ripe fresh Belgian goat cheese of your choice
1 jar of truffle honey
40 g of radish sprouts

TECHNIQUES: RAW, SAUCE

SUGGESTED BEVERAGE: TEMPRANILLO PURE RED (WINE CASTLE VANDEURZEN, BELGIUM)

SPRING

CHOCOLATE BROWNIE WITH TRUFFLE HONEY

4 SERVINGS

 5 MINUTES    VEGGIES    SMALL ROUND PLATE (WILD MOON)

RECIPE

Brownie:
Let the oven preheat to 180 °C.
Cut the beets into cubes and mix them finely. Melt the butter in a cooking pot over a low heat. Add the chocolate in pieces and let it melt gently.
Place the whole eggs, vanilla and sugar in a large, deep bowl and beat until you get a fluffy consistency. Add the beet puree, mix, then add the melted chocolate, a pinch of salt and the baking powder. Mix again.
Finally add the flour and mix thoroughly.
Line a square or rectangular baking pan with baking paper, pour in the dough and bake in the oven for 45 minutes.
Allow to cool completely before removing and cutting into squares.
Serve in paper molds if desired and decorate with chocolate chips.
Place a piece of brownie on each plate.
Drip some argan oil on it.

Serve:
Serve with a spoonful of truffle honey next to the brownie.

INGREDIENTS

400 g of cooked red organic beet

220 g black chocolate

125 g butter

240 g cane sugar

1 sachet of baking powder

3 eggs

1/2 teaspoon of vanilla powder

100 g pastry flour

pinch of salt (Verstegen)

1 jar of truffle honey

argan oil (Arqan)

TECHNIQUES: RAW, SAUCE

SUGGESTED BEVERAGE:
A CUP OF COFFEE

SUMMER

NUTRISCORE **A**

SUMMER

ROASTED LEEK TAGLIATELLE WITH MARJORAM, TURNIPS AND ARGAN OIL

4 SERVINGS

 20 MINUTES    VEGGIES    LARGE FLAT PLATE (WILD MOON)

RECIPE

Turnip puree:
Peel the turnips, cut them into pieces (keep 1 raw turnip whole).
Do the same with the onion.
Cook these together in boiling water with some sea salt.
Scoop the vegetables out of the cooking water and mix them together with some olive oil, black pepper and mace powder to create a smooth puree.
Spoon into a bowl and let it stiffen in the fridge.

Leek sauce:
Cut the green tops off the leek, about 1/3 of it, cut into pieces and wash it off well to remove all of the sand.
Boil the leek greens and a few marjoram leaves in water with sea salt until it looks done. Afterwards, remove the leek from the cooking liquid and cool it off under some tap water (this way you'll keep the beautiful green colour).
Puree these together with some cooking water, olive oil and some black pepper till you've made a nice sauce.

Leek tagliatelle:
Divide the bottom 2/3 leek into 2 separate parts. Afterwards, cut it lengthwise into strips of about 1 cm and then again until they are about the width of tagliatelle.
Make sure to wash the strips well in cold water and to dry them with some kitchen paper.
Place the final result into a metal bowl and char with a kitchen blow torch until the leek tagliatelle are light brown and feel soft.

Serve:
Place the roasted leek on the left-side of the plate.
Drizzle a few more drops of argan oil over them.
Top with a spoonful of caviar.
Place a spoonful of turnip puree on the right next to the leek and spread it out a bit, then dot the plate with the green leek sauce.
Garnish with some marjoram flowers and grated raw turnip.

INGREDIENTS

1 bunch young turnips
1 whole onion
coarse sea salt (Verstegen)
generous dash of olive oil (Iluigi)
black pepper (Verstegen)
mace powder (Verstegen)
1 leek
sprig fresh marjoram (with little flowers)
just a few drops of argan oil (Arqan)
100 g caviar

TECHNIQUES: MASHED POTATOES, SAUCE, ROAST, RAW
SUGGESTED BEVERAGE: WHITE WINE, CHARDONNAY (WINERY VALKE VLEUG, BELGIUM)

NUTRISCORE **A**

SUMMER

OPEN LASAGNE WITH WATERMELON, FENNEL CARPACCIO, DILL, BABY SPINACH, YELLOW CHERRY TOMATOES AND LEMON

4 SERVINGS

 15 MINUTES    VEGGIES    FRUITS    LARGE DEEP PLATE (WILD MOON)

RECIPE

Fennel carpaccio:
Slice the fennel paper thin with a sharp knife or mandoline.
Season with black pepper and sea salt, as well as some lemon juice and a dash of olive oil.
Leave to marinate for a few minutes.

Watermelon carpaccio:
Cut thin slices of watermelon and set them aside on a plate.

Serve:
Build up equal layers of marinated fennel and watermelon carpaccio over the 4 plates.
Cut yellow cherry tomatoes into slices and divide them between the fennel and the watermelon along with some small spinach leaves.
Spoon remaining marinade over. Finish by garnishing all of the plates with dill and sea fennel.
Finish with a few drops of fresh lemon juice and tasty olive oil.

INGREDIENTS

1 small fennel bulb
juice of 1 lemon
generous dash of olive oil (Iluigi)
black pepper (Verstegen)
coarse sea salt (Verstegen)
1 small watermelon (seedless)
12 yellow cherry tomatoes
handful of fresh baby spinach leaves
2 sprigs of fresh dill
1 cup of sea fennel (Koppert Cress)

TECHNIQUES: RAW, MARINATE   **SUGGESTED BEVERAGE:** ICED-TEA (WITHOUT ADDED SUGAR)

NUTRISCORE **A**

SUMMER

COLD WATERCRESS SOUP WITH HIPPO TOPS, REDCURRANTS AND ARGAN OIL

4 SERVINGS

 15 MINUTES    VEGGIES    MEDIUM BOWL (WILD MOON)

RECIPE

Watercress soup:

Peel, wash and chop the onion.
Wash watercress and cut stems from leaves.
Finely chop the stems.
Cook the stems together with the onion in a dash of argan oil.
Season with cayenne and sea salt and moisten with a dash of Super Kroon beer and some water.
Cover and braise gently for a few minutes.
Now add the watercress leaves, bring to the boil and puree everything in the blender.
Taste and season if necessary.
Place in the refrigerator.

Serve:

Divide the cold watercress soup over the 4 bowls.
Place a bunch of redcurrants in each, as well as some sprigs of Hippo Tops.
Finish with a few more drops of warmed argan oil for flavour.

INGREDIENTS

2 white onions
1 box watercress
argan oil (Arqan)
cayenne pepper
coarse sea salt
dash of Super Kroon beer (Brewery De Kroon)
4 bunches of ripe redcurrants
1 tray of Hippo Tops (Koppert Cress)

TECHNIQUES: RAW, SOUP   **SUGGESTED BEVERAGE:** SUPER KROON BEER (BREWERY DE KROON)

SUMMER

YELLOW CARROT AND CHERVIL SALAD WITH NORI, SESAME AND ICE TEA

4 SERVINGS

 20 MINUTES    VEGGIES    SERVING PLATE (WILD MOON)

RECIPE

Ice tea:
Let tea steep in 2 cups of water.
Pour through a sieve.
Place in the refrigerator.

Salad:
Wash, peel and cut yellow carrot into fine slices.
Then cut into threads.
Mix carrot with some fresh chervil and season with some sea salt, a few drops of lime juice and black pepper.

Serve:
Divide the salad over the 4 deep plates.
Pour some cold tea into the plates.
Cut the nori into strands of about 5 cm and place some threads on each salad.
Sprinkle with some sesame seeds.
Garnish with chopped cress and a few more drops of warmed argan oil for flavour.

INGREDIENTS

loose black or green tea of your choice
4 yellow carrots
40 g fresh chervil
coarse sea salt
juice of 1 lime
black pepper (Verstegen)
1 sheet of nori
black sesame seeds
1 cup of Ghoa Cress (Koppert Cress)
argan oil (Arqan)

TECHNIQUES: RAW, BOUILLON, ROAST   **SUGGESTED BEVERAGE:** SPARKLING WINE (WINERY VALKE VLEUG, BELGIUM)

SUMMER

SWEET PEPPER CAVIAR WITH MARJORAM, GREEN OLIVES, BURRATA FLAKES AND ACLLA CRESS

4 SERVINGS

 20 MINUTES  VEGGIES  SERVING PLATE (WILD MOON)

RECIPE

Parchment:
Cut wafer-thin slices of yellow sweet pepper.
Grease an oven tray with olive oil or use a baking cloth.
Place the raw pepper chips side-by-side on the tray and season with sea salt and black pepper.
Place these in an oven at 100 °C for 30 to 40 minutes until crispy.

Caviar:
Clean, wash and cut all remaining peppers into a fine brunoise.
Cut some green olives into fine brunoise.
Briefly fry everything until soft and crispy in a dash of olive oil.
Season with black pepper and sea salt.
Add finely chopped marjoram and mix. Allow to cool.

Serve:
Divide the cold pepper-olive caviar over the 4 bowls.
Tear the burrata into flakes and divide evenly over the caviar.
Garnish with whole olives and a few sprigs of cress.
Top with a few more drops of olive oil, coarse sea salt and black pepper on the burrata. Add a few spoonfuls of Légumaise.
Finish with a few drops of fresh lemon juice and tasty olive oil.

INGREDIENTS

1 yellow sweet pepper
1 red sweet pepper
coarse sea salt
black pepper
jar of pitted green olives
2 sprigs of fresh marjoram
1 fresh burrata
1 tray of Aclla Cress (Koppert Cress)
olive oil (Iluigi)
150 g Bio Légumaise Provence, paprika with thyme

TECHNIQUES: CAVIAR, RAW, STEW, MARINATE, PARCHMENT, EMULSION

SUGGESTED BEVERAGE: WHITE WINE, PINOT AUXERROIS (WINERY VALKE VLEUG, BELGIUM)

NUTRISCORE **B**

SUMMER

CUCUMBER LASAGNE WITH RASPBERRY, LEMON VERBENA, LEMON JUICE AND ILUIGI'S OLIVE ICE CREAM

4 SERVINGS

 15 MINUTES    VEGGIES    FRUITS    MEDIUM FLAT PLATE (WILD MOON)

RECIPE

Cucumber lasagne:
Peel the cucumber.
Make wafer-thin discs with the help of a mandoline or vegetable peeler. Drizzle the cucumber slices with lemon juice. Marinate for a few minutes.

Serve:
Place the marinated cucumber slices on the plates, 3 per plate and arrange 5 raspberries around the cucumber slices on each plate. Now place a spoonful of creamy olive ice cream on top and garnish with a few lemon verbena leaves.
Finish with a few more drops of olive oil and freshly grated lemon zest.

INGREDIENTS

1 small cucumber

20 ripe raspberries

1 container of olive ice cream (Iluigi)

2 sprigs of fresh lemon verbena

olive oil (Iluigi)

zest from 1 lemon

TECHNIQUES: RAW, MARINATE, ICE CREAM

SUGGESTED BEVERAGE: POTATO VODKA MOJITO (WITHOUT ADDED SUGARS)

EVER HEARD OF OLIVE ICE CREAM?

We have already written about the health benefits of olive oil, but have you ever heard of olive ice cream? This is probably a combination that you wouldn't think of straight away. Still, olive oil ice cream has been around for a while and it has a unique and delicious taste and a more creamy structure. We can recommend **Iluigi** as the top brand for artisan olive ice cream.

SUMMER

APRICOT MARMALADE WITH LAVENDER, FRESH YOGURT, OLIVE OIL AND LIMON CRESS

4 SERVINGS

 15 MINUTES    VEGGIES    FRUITS    SMALL BOWL (WILD MOON)

RECIPE

Marmalade:
Cut 7 apricots in half, pit and cut into large pieces.
Cover and stew slowly with a few lavender flowers.
Stir occasionally so that they do not burn until they form a nice, unsweetened, creamy marmalade.

Lavender water:
Place a few sprigs of lavender with flowers in a carafe of ice-cold water.
Leave to marinate and pour as a cool drink to serve with this dish.

Serve:
Divide the marmalade over the 4 bowls.
Place an ample spoonful of yogurt in the centre.
Cut the 8th apricot into slices and top the yogurt with the apricot slices.
Garnish with the cut cress and finish with a few more drops of high-quality olive oil.

INGREDIENTS

8 ripe apricots
sprigs of fresh lavender
1 litre of water of your choice
1 pot of Fresh yogurt
1 cup of Limon Cress (Koppert Cress)
olive oil (Iluigi)

TECHNIQUES:
RAW, STEW, MARMALADE, MARINATE

SUGGESTED BEVERAGE:
LAVENDER SCENTED WATER

SPAGHETTI WITH YELLOW COURGETTE, BABY SPINACH AND WILD GARLIC, MOTTI CRESS AND TOASTED BREAD TOPPING

4 SERVINGS

20 MINUTES · VEGGIES · LARGE PLATE (WILD MOON)

RECIPE

Bread topping:
Crush the toasted bread into crumbs.
Put a dash of olive oil in the pan, heat up and add the bread crumbs.
Brown over low heat. Season lightly with some sea salt.

Spaghetti:
Cook spaghetti in boiling water with sea salt for 4 minutes.
Drain and toss with some olive oil and black pepper.
Wash the yellow courgette, cut into 2 mm slices using a slicer.
Then cut into long spaghetti strands.
Finely chop the wild garlic and spinach.
Fry the vegetables with some olive oil for a few minutes without allowing them to brown. Season with sea salt and black pepper.
Now add the pasta and mix well.

Serve:
Divide the warm spaghetti mix over the 4 plates and top with some toasted bread crumbs and the lemon zest.
Drizzle with some cold olive oil and garnish with the cut cress.

INGREDIENTS

2 slices of toasted bread
olive oil (Iluigi)
sea salt (Verstegen)
250 g fresh spaghetti
black pepper (Verstegen)
1 yellow courgette
2 wild garlic leaves
20 g fresh young spinach
1 cup of Motti Cress (Koppert Cress)
lemon zest

TECHNIQUES:
RAW, FRY, BOIL, TOAST

SUGGESTED BEVERAGE:
RED WINE, PINOT NOIR
(WINERY VALKE VLEUG, BELGIUM)

SUMMER

PATTYPAN SQUASH BURGERS WITH MOZZARELLA, ROASTED LEEK AND FRESH THYME

4 SERVINGS

 20 MINUTES    VEGGIES    LARGE FLAT PLATE (WILD MOON)

RECIPE

Roast the leeks:
Clean, wash and cut the leeks into 5 cm julienne.
Place in ice cold water.
The leek strips will become firmer and more brittle.
Drain, dry with kitchen paper and place in metal container.
Roast the leek strips with a kitchen blow torch, shaking them frequently so that the colour is even.
Then drizzle with a dash of olive oil and season with sea salt.

Hamburgers:
Wash the pattypan squash. Cut them in half across the middle.
Fry them on both sides in a pan with some olive oil.
Season with black pepper and sea salt, as well as with some washed and finely chopped fresh thyme.
Cook until they are lightly browned and still crisp.
Cut the mozzarella into 16 equal slices. Now assemble the burgers:
- Take a bottom pattypan piece
- Place a slice of mozzarella on top
- Add some roasted leeks
- Now put the top pattypan on and attach everything together from the top with a cocktail stick.

Place in a warm oven or on the BBQ until the mozzarella starts to melt. Serve.

Serve:
Place a circle of Légumaise on each plate.
Place 2 yellow and 2 green warm, pattypan hamburgers on each plate.
Garnish with some sprigs of fresh thyme and a dusting of black pepper, then drizzle some olive oil over each plate.

INGREDIENTS

1 baby leek
olive oil (Iluigi)
16 mini pattypan (also patisson) squash (yellow & green)
200 g mozzarella
a few sprigs of fresh thyme
150 g Bio Légumaise Bilbao, yellow paprika with lemon
16 bamboo or wooden cocktail sticks
black pepper (Verstegen)
sea salt (Verstegen)

TECHNIQUES: ROAST, EMULSION, BAKE

SUGGESTED BEVERAGE: DELVAUX BEER (BREWERY DE KROON, BELGIUM)

NUTRISCORE **A**

SUMMER

CUCUMBER SALAD WITH THAI BASIL, SHALLOT, LIME, RED CHILLI, ROASTED PEANUTS AND SYRHA LEAVES

4 SERVINGS

 15 MINUTES    VEGGIES    NOTEN    SMALL BOWL (WILD MOON)

RECIPE

Cucumber:
Peel the cucumber.
Cut it in half lengthwise and scoop out the seeds with a spoon.
Mix the seeds with some lime juice and olive oil to make a sauce.
Season with some sea salt.
Cut the cucumber into halfmoons about .5 cm thick.
Remove the spicy seeds and then chop a piece of red chilli.
Stew the cucumber with the chilli very briefly with some olive oil and sea salt. Allow to cool.
Finely chop a few leaves of Thai basil and mix with the cucumber salad together with the sauce.

Prepare garnish:
Finely chop shallot and season with some sea salt.
Marinate a little. Coarsely chop the roasted peanuts.

Serve:
Place the Syrha Leaves in each bowl.
Top with the cucumber salad.
Garnish with shallot and peanut.
Drizzle some more olive oil over it.

INGREDIENTS

1 cucumber
juice of 1 lime
olive oil (Iluigi)
coarse sea salt
1 red chilli
2 sprigs of Thai basil
2 shallots
40 g roasted peanuts
1 tray of Syrha Leaves (Koppert Cress)

TECHNIQUES: STEWING, RAW, ROASTING, MARINATING   **SUGGESTED BEVERAGE:** JOB BEER (BREWERY DE KROON, BELGIUM)

A CARPET OF VITAMINS!

Cresses are mini vegetables. They are also called the new vegetables or 'living vegetables'. Why? Cresses are the beginning of a plant's development. These have up to 10 times more nutrients than a fully grown plant and are super healthy. Its use in dishes is therefore encouraged. In addition, due to the wide range of flavors available on the market, you can match them perfectly with your culinary creation. In addition to health, they also add an extra flavor dimension to a dish and certainly also a visual touch! Definitely try this! We are already convinced.

DO YOU KNOW THE BENEFITS OF LIVING VEGETABLES?

In recent years, we have seen cresses — fresh young plants — widely used within the culinary world. There is a solid reason for this: not only are there many different types, which each feature a unique flavour and aroma, but they also really finish a dish visually.

But, most importantly, cresses are super healthy! Cresses are also known as 'living vegetables'. We owe all this to Rob Baan, a pioneer in the vegetable world who — like Frank Fol — aims to help people live healthier lives rich with flavour. With **Koppert Cress**, he offers the most innovative, natural ingredients for a unique flavour sensation.

SUMMER

FRESH CHERRIES WITH COTTAGE CHEESE, FRESH LEMON BALM, HONEY AND APPLE BLOSSOMS

4 SERVINGS

 10 MINUTES  VEGGIES  FRUITS   SMALL FLAT PLATE (WILD MOON)

RECIPE

Quark mix:
Mix the fresh quark with the finely chopped lemon balm.
Marinate for a few minutes.

Serve:
Place the soft quark on each plate and shape into a circle.
Place the cherries on top as you wish.
Top with some fresh artisan honey and the Apple Blossoms.

INGREDIENTS

jar of fresh quark
2 sprigs of fresh lemon balm
250 g large sweet cherries
4 tablespoons of runny artisan honey
1 cup of Apple Blossoms (Koppert Cress)

TECHNIQUES:
RAW, MARINATE

SUGGESTED BEVERAGE:
HOT TEA (WITHOUT ADDED SUGARS)

SUMMER

BITTER CHOCOLATE CHUNKS WITH OLIVE OIL, COARSE SEA SALT AND LIMON CRESS

4 SERVINGS

 5 MINUTES  VEGGIES  SMALL FLAT PLATE (WILD MOON)

RECIPE

Preparation:
Break the chocolate in uneven chunks.
Place them on a plate.

Serve:
Drizzle a little olive oil over the chocolate and sprinkle with a little coarse sea salt.
Garnish with the Limon Cress.

INGREDIENTS

piece of bitter dark chocolate
drops of olive oil (Iluigi)
coarse sea salt (Verstegen)
1 cup of Limon Cress (Koppert Cress)

TECHNIQUES:
RAW

SUGGESTED BEVERAGE:
A CUP OF COFFE

NUTRISCORE **E**

NUTRISCORE **B**

BRAISED SPRING ONION WITH LEMON VERBENA, PAPRIKA AND FLAX SEEDS

4 SERVINGS

 15 MINUTES    VEGGIES    FLAT PLATE (WILD MOON)

RECIPE

Spring onion:
Hand wash the spring onions until clean.
Put a dash of olive oil and a generous dash of water in a stew pot together.
Put the spring onions inside and season with some sea salt and pepper. Cover and braise over low heat for about 10 minutes.

Serve:
Put 3 spring onions per plate in a circle.
Place a spoonful of Bio Légumaise in the middle.
Finish with some drops of olive oil, lemon zest, some flax seeds, a few lemon verbena leaves on top and some rapeseed flowers.

INGREDIENTS

1 bunch of spring onions
olive oil (Iluigi)
sea salt (Verstegen)
freshly ground black pepper
150 g Bio Légumaise Provence, paprika with thyme
lemon zest
a few flax seeds
2 sprigs lemon verbena
rapeseed flowers

TECHNIQUES:
BRAISE, RAW, EMULSION

SUGGESTED BEVERAGE:
PINOT AUXERROIS
(WINERY VALKE VLEUG, BELGIUM)

WHAT ABOUT HEALTHY SAUCES WITH A VEGETABLE BASE?

Europeans are sauce eaters. It's in our genes. Usually they are unhealthy. What if we could eat as much sauce as we wanted? And increase our vegetable intake in a tasty way? Well, we have the solution for you: Légumaises! These delicacies include a limited percentage of rapeseed oil — one of the healthiest oils by the way — and are made from cooked vegetable blends, each with a pronounced flavour. You can eat them cold but also heat them up. Now they're also available in a BIO version! Want to check it out?

AUTUMN

AUTUMN

FORK-CRUSHED POTATOES AND CHESTNUT MUSHROOM CARPACCIO WITH MOTTI CRESS AND CELERY SAUCE

4 SERVINGS

 20 MINUTES    VEGGIES    LARGE FLAT PLATE (WILD MOON)

RECIPE

Crushed potatoes:
Peel the potatoes and cook them with the pressed garlic in salted water.
Drain, crush with a fork and keep warm under a lid.

Celery sauce:
Cut about half of the celery (with leafy green tops) into pieces and wash well so that any dirt or grit is removed.
Braise the celery in water with coarse sea salt until tender, remove it from the cooking liquid (reserve the cooking liquid) and cool under running water (so that it retains its beautiful green colour).
Blend it together with the cooking liquid, olive oil and black pepper into a smooth-flowing sauce.

Celery pieces:
Cut the remaining celery into small pieces and wash well so that any dirt or grit is removed.
Cook the celery in the boiling water until tender-crisp.
Remove the celery from the cooking liquid and cool under running water.

Carpaccio:
Cut the chestnut mushrooms into thin slices.

Serve:
Divide the lukewarm potatoes evenly over the plates.
Spoon the tender-crisp celery over the potatoes and drizzle everything with olive oil.
Arrange the mushroom slices on top and season with black pepper and sea salt.
Spoon some sauce over the plates and garnish with the cress.

INGREDIENTS

800 g waxy potatoes
2 garlic cloves
coarse sea salt (Verstegen)
400 g green celery
olive oil (Iluigi)
black pepper (Verstegen)
4 to 6 chestnut mushrooms
Motti Cress (Koppert Cress)

TECHNIQUES: BRAISE, SAUCE, RAW   **SUGGESTED BEVERAGE:** GAMAY RED WINE (WINERY VALKE VLEUG, BELGIUM)

NUTRISCORE **A**

AUTUMN

CHARD SPAGHETTI WITH SHIITAKE, CASHEW NUTS AND CITRA LEAVES

4 SERVINGS

 20 MINUTES    VEGGIES   NUTS    LARGE FLAT PLATE (WILD MOON)

RECIPE

Spaghetti:
Wash and cut 600 g of chard (leaf and stalk) into a fine julienne. Sauté everything in a little bit of butter until crispy, with a splash of water, coarse sea salt, pepper and mace powder.

Sauce:
Cut the remaining 200 g of chard (stalks only), shiitake, shallot, garlic and cashew nuts into small dice and cook gently in some butter. Season with coarse sea salt and mace.
When everything is nicely done, mix in the légumaise.

Serve:
Divide the warm chard spaghetti evenly over the plates. Spoon the sauce on top and drizzle everything with a little argan oil. Now sprinkle with some of the grated cheese and garnish with the Citra Leaves.

INGREDIENTS

800 g chard (red and yellow)
coarse sea salt (Verstegen)
black pepper (Verstegen)
mace powder (Verstegen)
200 g shiitake mushrooms
2 shallots
2 cloves garlic
80 g cashew nuts
butter
150 g Bio Légumaise Vietnam, celeriac with curry
a few drops of argan oil (Arqan)
piece of Brugge Old cheese
1 cup of Citra Leaves (Koppert Cress)

TECHNIQUES:
SAUTÉ, SAUCE, RAW

SUGGESTED BEVERAGE:
PINOT NOIR (WINERY VALKE VLEUG, BELGIUM)

AUTUMN

KOHLRABI RAVIOLI AND PURPLE CAULIFLOWER WITH HAZELNUTS AND JASMINE BLOSSOMS

4 SERVINGS

30 MINUTES · VEGGIES · NUTS · LARGE FLAT PLATE (WILD MOON)

RECIPE

Ravioli:
Peel the kohlrabi. Cut it in half.
Use a mandoline to cut 8 very thin round slices (as large as possible), 1 mm thick.
For the ravioli, blanch these slices one by one in boiling water with some sea salt, for 30 seconds.
Remove with a skimmer and cool in cold water.

Filling:
Dice the remaining kohlrabi, shallot and 200 g of cauliflower into a brunoise.
Sauté in a bit of rapeseed oil until crispy.
Season with sea salt and pepper.
Fill each ravioli slice with the warm vegetable mixture and place on a large plate.
Microwave them briefly to reheat.

Garnish:
Chop the hazelnuts.
Slice the remaining raw purple cauliflower.

Serve:
Place 2 warm ravioli on each (hot) plate.
Spoon some hot Légumaise on top in the middle.
Garnish with the hazelnuts and crispy cauliflower.
Drizzle everything with some argan oil and top with a few Jasmine Blossoms.

TECHNIQUES: BLANCH, SAUCE, SAUTÉ, RAW

SUGGESTED BEVERAGE: DELVAUX BEER (BREWERY DE KROON, BELGIUM)

INGREDIENTS

1 large kohlrabi
coarse sea salt
1 shallot
1 small purple cauliflower
rapeseed oil
black pepper
60 g hazelnuts
150 g Bio Légumaise Périgord, mushroom with truffle
argan oil (Arqan)
Jasmine Blossoms (Koppert Cress)

NUTRISCORE A

AUTUMN

BRAISED CARROT WITH GINGER, GREEN ASPARAGUS, LIME AND SUNFLOWER SEEDS

4 SERVINGS

 20 MINUTES  VEGGIES  MEDIUM BOWL (WILD MOON)

RECIPE

Asparagus:
Peel asparagus and cut diagonally into equal pieces.
Briefly blanch the asparagus in salted water.

Stir-fry:
Peel carrots. Cut diagonally into equal pieces. Keep the greens.
Put some olive oil in the wok and slowly stir-fry the carrots together with thinly sliced red chilli and freshly grated ginger until crisp.
Add the asparagus, season with ras el hanout and some coarse sea salt if desired.
Add the lime juice and stir well.

Serve:
Divide the stir-fry evenly over the bowls.
Garnish with sunflower seeds and some sprigs of carrot greens.

INGREDIENTS

1 bunch green asparagus
coarse sea salt (Verstegen)
500 g carrot with greens
olive oil (Iluigi)
piece of red chilli
piece of fresh ginger
ras el hanout spice blend (Verstegen)
juice of 1 lime
60 g sunflower seeds

TECHNIQUES:
BLANCH, STIR-FRY, RAW

SUGGESTED BEVERAGE:
DELVAUX BEER
(BREWERY DE KROON, BELGIUM)

HOW TO EAT PLANT-BASED IN AUTUMN?

Autumn is for many a typical period for eating wild. But this season brings a lot more than you would think. We started with mushrooms, celery, grapes, truffle, turnip, chard, shallot, broccoli, kohlrabi, sweet potato, nuts, carrot, cress, purple cauliflower, fresh herbs, radish, etc. ... But autumn offers so much more. Just think of the many types of cabbage, citrus fruits, beets, pumpkin, etc. ... So it shouldn't be a problem to indulge yourself in 100% vegetables. Long live autumn!

AUTUMN

ROASTED ONION STEW WITH CHESTNUT MUSHROOM, SAVORY AND GRATED RADISH

4 SERVINGS

 30 MINUTES    VEGGIES    LARGE DEEP PLATE (WILD MOON)

RECIPE

Stew:
Peel the onions and garlic.
Chop them together with 4 mushrooms and brown them in some butter.
Season with sea salt and black pepper and add some fresh savory.
Then moisten with the beer and some water.
Stew covered for 10 minutes.
Blend everything into a smooth sauce and then add the remaining 12 mushrooms.
Cover and cook for another 10 minutes.

Serve:
Place 3 cooked mushrooms in each deep plate and spoon the thick, hot sauce on top.
Now grate some raw radish over the top and garnish with a few drops of argan oil and some Daikon Cress.

INGREDIENTS

6 onions
2 garlic cloves
16 large chestnut mushrooms
butter
coarse sea salt
freshly ground black pepper
2 sprigs of savory
1 bottle of beer Super Kroon (Brewery De Kroon)
1 small white radish
argan oil (Arqan)
Daikon Cress (Koppert Cress)

TECHNIQUES: SAUCE, STEW, RAW

SUGGESTED BEVERAGE: SUPER KROON BEER (BREWERY DE KROON, BELGIUM)

WHAT IS BEER & FOOD PAIRING?

Belgium is a beer country par excellence. Our country, therefore, has many small and larger breweries. Still, beer is not yet getting the place it deserves in culinary terms! Because the right choice of beer for a certain dish can actually work wonders. The fruitiness, depth, bitterness, freshness and finesse of a beer, therefore, determine in which culinary creation it is best served and of course enjoyed. In *Wild Cooking* the beers of **Brewery De Kroon** inspired us.

NUTRISCORE **A**

AUTUMN

RIGATONI WITH BROCCOLI PESTO, LEMON, ROASTED RED ONION, FRESH APRICOTS AND JASMINE BLOSSOMS

4 SERVINGS

 20 MINUTES  VEGGIES NUTS  MEDIUM BOWL (WILD MOON)

RECIPE

Pesto:
Chop some raw broccoli florets to the texture of crumbs and reserve for topping. Boil broccoli briefly in salted water. Then remove the broccoli, cool under cold running water and set the cooking liquid aside.
Now blend the cooked broccoli with a handful of basil, grated cheese, almonds, olive oil, some of the cooking liquid, sea salt and black pepper until it forms a delicious creamy pesto.

Pasta:
Cook pasta in briskly boiling salted water according to package instructions.
Drain and stir into the pesto with some lemon juice and lemon zest.

Garnish:
Remove the pits from the apricots and cut into cubes.
Peel the red onion, cut into wedges, and place in a flame-resistant dish. Then place the dish on a wooden chopping board and roast the onions with a kitchen blow torch until they are lightly coloured all over.
This process also cooks the onions.

Serve:
Spoon the hot pasta into the bowls.
Sprinkle the apricot cubes, roasted onion slices and the broccoli floret crumbs over the pasta.
Garnish with some Jasmine Blossoms.

INGREDIENTS

1 small head of broccoli
coarse sea salt
fresh basil
40 g Brugge Old cheese
40 g almonds (blanched)
olive oil (Iluigi)
freshly-ground black pepper
rigatoni pasta
juice and zest of 1 lemon
2 apricots
1 to 2 red onions
Jasmine Blossoms
(Koppert Cress)

TECHNIQUES: SAUCE, ROAST, RAW

SUGGESTED BEVERAGE: WHITE WINE, AUXERROIS (WINERY VALKE VLEUG, BELGIUM)

AUTUMN

CRUSHED STRAWBERRY WITH GINGER, COURGETTE, PISTACHIO ICE CREAM AND LIMON CRESS

4 SERVINGS

 15 MINUTES  VEGGIES  FRUITS NUTS  MEDIUM BOWL (WILD MOON)

RECIPE

Strawberry courgette:
Wash strawberries, dry and then hull them.
Crush lightly with fork.
Julienne the courgette.
Mix raw with strawberry and some grated ginger.

Serve:
Spoon the strawberry-courgette mixture into the bowls.
Place a scoop of pistachio ice cream in each bowl.
Garnish with the coarsely chopped pistachios, a few drops of olive oil and some Limon Cress.

INGREDIENTS

250 g strawberries
1 small green courgette
piece of fresh ginger
pistachio ice cream (Iluigi)
fresh pistachio nuts
olive oil (Iluigi)
Limon Cress (Koppert Cress)

TECHNIQUES: SAUCE, RAW   **SUGGESTED BEVERAGE:** WATER INFUSED WITH GINGER

NUTRISCORE B

AUTUMN

RADISH VERMICELLI WITH FRESH GOAT CHEESE, ROASTED BUCKWHEAT, LÉGUMAISE ITALIA AND ADJI CRESS

4 SERVINGS

20 MINUTES   VEGGIES   LARGE COLOURFUL DEEP PLATE (WILD MOON)

RECIPE

Vermicelli:
Peel the radish. Cut it into wafer-thin slices using a vegetable peeler.
Now cut into fine vermicelli.
Season with sea salt and white wine vinegar.
Leave to marinate a little.

Serve:
Place a spoonful of légumaise on one side of each plate.
Add the marinated radish vermicelli.
Place pieces of goat cheese and some black pepper on top of the Légumaise.
Finish with roasted buckwheat, a few drops of argan oil and Adji Cress on the vermicelli.

INGREDIENTS

1 small white radish
coarse sea salt (Verstegen)
white wine vinegar
Bio Légumaise Italia, tomato with basil
160 g fresh goat cheese
freshly ground black pepper (Verstegen)
roasted buckwheat
argan oil (Arqan)
Adji Cress (Koppert Cress)

TECHNIQUES:
MARINATING, EMULSION, ROASTING, RAW

SUGGESTED BEVERAGE:
JOB BEER
(BREWERY DE KROON, BELGIUM)

AUTUMN

SALAD OF GREEN GRAPES AND SWEET POTATO, BLACK SESAME, DILL, LIME, YELLOW CHERRY TOMATO AND ANISE BLOSSOMS

4 SERVINGS

 25 MINUTES  VEGGIES  FRUITS  MEDIUM PLATE (WILD MOON)

RECIPE

Salad:
Peel the sweet potatoes, cut into cubes and cook in salted water.
Remove from the heat and leave to cool.
Cut the grapes and cherry tomatoes into halves.
Season with sea salt, black pepper, olive oil and lime juice.
Mix everything and leave to marinate.

Serve:
Place the salad mix on each plate.
Drizzle some olive oil over it and sprinkle with black sesame seeds.
Garnish with sprigs of fresh dill and some Anise Blossoms.

INGREDIENTS

2 sweet potatoes
coarse sea salt (Verstegen)
small bunch of green seedless grapes
package of yellow cherry tomatoes
freshly ground black pepper (Verstegen)
olive oil (Iluigi)
juice of 1 lime
black sesame seeds
a few sprigs of fresh dill
Anise Blossoms (Koppert Cress)

TECHNIQUES:
COOKING, RAW

SUGGESTED BEVERAGE:
WHITE WINE, AUXERROIS
(WINERY VALKE VLEUG, BELGIUM)

NUTRISCORE C

AUTUMN

BRAISED CELERY STICKS WITH CREAMY POTATOES, GOAT CHEESE AND CAVIAR

4 SERVINGS

 25 MINUTES    VEGGIES    LARGE COLOURED PLATE (WILD MOON)

RECIPE

Celery sticks:
Cut the celery into equal sticks, 7 cm long and 5 mm wide.
Place them in a cooking pot with some butter and water.
Season with sea salt and cayenne pepper.
Braise until tender-crisp and leave to cool in the cooking liquid.

Hot potato salad:
Peel the potatoes, cut into cubes and boil in salted water.
Drain and mix warm with cayenne pepper, fresh goat cheese and a few leaves of finely chopped Oyster Leaves.

Serve:
Place some hot potato salad on each plate and then add some warm celery sticks.
Top with a spoonful of caviar, some of the celery cooking liquid and garnish with finely chopped Oyster Leaves.

INGREDIENTS

1 bunch white celery
butter
sea salt (Verstegen)
cayenne pepper (Verstegen)
300 g boiling potatoes
4 tablespoons fresh goat cheese
Oyster Leaves (Koppert Cress)
100 g caviar

TECHNIQUES: BRAISE, BOIL, RAW

SUGGESTED BEVERAGE: POTATO VODKA (BELGIAN SECRETS)

HOW DO YOU USE FISHPEARLS?

Yes, we are indeed talking about caviar! Yes, this is a luxury item, but a very tasty one for sure. If you have the chance to taste it, it is important to serve caviar in its most optimal form. Slurping it off the back of your hand, or adding a spoon of caviar on top of a dish to get an extra dimension or the ultimate taste experience with a warm potato preparation. In all 3 cases, you will notice that the warmth of the hand or dish makes the caviar's flavour shine. It is very important to never ever heat the caviar, that would be a shame, for you and for the caviar!

AUTUMN

SHALLOT WITH TURMERIC, CAULIFLOWER AND CUCUMBER WITH CURRY

4 SERVINGS

 25 MINUTES  VEGGIES  LARGE PLATE (WILD MOON)

RECIPE

Shallots:

Boil water and season with coarse sea salt, cayenne pepper and a fair amount of turmeric powder.
Cover and simmer the shallots in this stock for 20 minutes.
Remove from the water and drain on kitchen paper.
Now fry the shallots in olive oil until light brown on both sides and season with coarse sea salt.

Garnish:

Cut small florets from the cauliflower.
Cut cucumber into small, attractive triangular wedges.

Serve:

Make a ring of Légumaise on each plate.
Arrange the cauliflower and cucumber around the ring of sauce.
Place 2 hot shallots in the centre of each ring.
Sprinkle some flowers and a few drops of olive oil on top, dust with a bit of turmeric powder and garnish with chives.

INGREDIENTS

coarse sea salt (Verstegen)
cayenne pepper (Verstegen)
turmeric powder (Verstegen)
8 large shallots
olive oil (Iluigi)
1 piece of raw cauliflower
2 mini (baby) cucumbers
Bio Légumaise Vietnam, celeriac with curry
herbal flowers (marjoram, chives, savory, ...)
fresh chives

TECHNIQUES: EMULSION, RAW, BOIL, FRY

SUGGESTED BEVERAGE: WHITE WINE, CHARDONNAY (WINERY VALKE VLEUG, BELGIUM)

WHAT ABOUT BIO?

Choosing BIO or organic is not only a lifestyle choice but it's also choosing better health! Wild Cooking wants to make a statement: If you can, you certainly shouldn't hesitate to choose bio or organic. Why?

- Pure food
- Healthy
- Good for the environment
- Animal friendly
- 100% the future

In order to support BIO cultivation, we need to give assurances to agriculture about the path that the decline and consumption will follow. We want to support the farmers who make the switch. If you want to enjoy organic meals at home, we have a great tip for you! Please visit **www.ekomenu.be.** Bon Appetit!

WINTER

NUTRISCORE **A**

WINTER

CELERIAC GRILLED OVER AN OPEN FIRE WITH GOMASIO, ROSEMARY, VINAIGRETTE OF PINK GRAPEFRUIT, CRANBERRIES AND GHOA CRESS

4 SERVINGS

 BETWEEN 90 AND 120 MINUTES    VEGGIES    FRUITS    LARGE FLAT PLATE (WILD MOON)

RECIPE

Celeriac:
Wash, dry and rub celeriac with argan oil. Season with gomasio.
Place on the grill and turn regularly so that it cooks evenly.
Take a bunch of fresh rosemary.
Put some olive oil in a jar and dip the rosemary in it, now use this 'brush' to regularly baste the celeriac on all sides.
The cooking of the celeriac can take up to 2 hours depending on its thickness.

Vinaigrette:
Stew the fresh (or frozen) cranberries in some olive oil until they form a compote. Now add some grapefruit zest and juice.
Mix everything into a beautiful, pink, runny vinaigrette.

Celeriac emulsion:
When celeriac is cooked, peel off outer skin with a knife.
Cut 4 slices to place on the plates.
Cut the rest into chunks and blend it, together with a splash of water, a good splash of olive oil, a sprig of finely chopped rosemary, black pepper and sea salt into a smooth emulsion.

Serve:
Spread an oval of warm celeriac emulsion on each plate and then add a disc of cooked celeriac.
Spoon some vinaigrette over the preparation.
Garnish with some extra gomasio, dried cranberries and a few sprigs of Ghoa Cress.

INGREDIENTS

1 small celeriac root (whole)
argan oil (Arqan)
gomasio classic (Verstegen)
a few branches of fresh rosemary
strong dash of olive oil (Iluigi)
100 g fresh or frozen cranberries
zest and juice of 1 pink grapefruit
freshly ground black pepper (Verstegen)
freshly ground sea salt (Verstegen)
120 g dried cranberries
1 cup of Ghoa Cress (Koppert Cress)

TECHNIQUES: GRILL, SAUCE, RAW, DRY, EMULSION

SUGGESTED BEVERAGE: JOB BEER (BREWERY DE KROON, BELGIUM)

NUTRISCORE **A**

WINTER

WHITE CABBAGE TAGLIATELLE, MASHED RED CABBAGE, HAZELNUT, PUMPERNICKEL BREAD CRUSTS AND LUPINE CRESS

4 SERVINGS

 30 MINUTES  VEGGIES   NUTS  LARGE FLAT PLATE (WILD MOON)

RECIPE

Red cabbage:
Chop red cabbage and garlic finely.
Stew with a knob of butter but don't allow to brown.
Peel potatoes, cut into pieces and wash.
Add potato and bay leaf to the red cabbage and add water to cover 2/3.
Season everything with mace, sea salt and black pepper.
Cover and stew until the potato is tender.
Drain some cooking water, not all.
Remove bay leaf and stir the mash until well blended.

White cabbage:
Remove the outer leaves and wash the cabbage.
Then cut the white cabbage into strips of about 1 cm, a handful per person.
Stir-fry this until crispy in a little butter and season well with pepper and sea salt.
Add some water and stir thoroughly. Lightly brown.

Pumpernickel croutons:
Cut the slices of pumpernickel bread in half and then into equal strips.
Fry these in the pan until they are slightly crispy.

Serve:
Spoon an abundant scoop of warm mash into the centre of each plate.
Divide some stir-fried white cabbage ribbons over this.
Spoon some butter from the pan around each preparation.
Garnish with the pumpernickel croutons, the Lupine Cress and some chopped roasted hazelnuts.

TECHNIQUES: STIR-FRY, STEW, ROAST, RAW

SUGGESTED BEVERAGE: TEMPRANILLO, PURE RED
(WINE CASTLE VANDEURZEN, BELGIUM)

INGREDIENTS

1 small red cabbage
2 cloves of peeled garlic
butter
1 kg soft boiling potatoes
bay leaf (Verstegen)
mace powder (Verstegen)
coarse sea salt (Verstegen)
black pepper (Verstegen)
1 small white cabbage
2 slices of pumpernickel bread
1 cup of Lupine Cress (Koppert Cress)
roasted hazelnuts

WINTER

TURNIP ROYAL WITH KYONA MUSTARD CRESS

4 SERVINGS

 30 MINUTES  VEGGIES  LARGE FLAT PLATE (WILD MOON)

RECIPE

Turnips:
Clean and wash the turnips.
Keep the most beautiful green leaves. Peel the turnips.

We prepare them in 3 ways:

1. Grilled discs
Cut 3 slices per person, thickness 1 cm, cut from the thickest part of the turnip.
Season with salt and pepper and a few drops of argan oil.
Grill slowly on both sides. Set aside.

2. Sour threads
Cut some wafer-thin slices from the remaining turnip parts with a mandoline.
Then cut those into strands with a sharp knife.
Marinate these in mixture of half water, half apple vinegar.
Also, add some salt and let it rest for 30 minutes.

3. Emulsion
Cut the remaining turnip pieces into cubes and cook them in lightly-salted water.
Add a few finely chopped green leaves and cook for another 30 seconds. Then blend turnip with greens and a dash of cooking liquid, add a little mace and a dash of argan oil.
Add more pepper and sea salt if desired.

Serve:
Place 3 hot discs on each plate.
Spoon some fresh green turnip emulsion onto each slice.
Drain slightly tart turnip julienne and place a small heap on each slice.
Now garnish with some finely chopped chives and Kyona Mustard Cress. Add a few more drops of argan oil if desired.

INGREDIENTS

4 larger turnips with green tops
black pepper (Verstegen)
coarse sea salt (Verstegen)
argan oil (Arqan)
apple vinegar
mace powder (Verstegen)
a few sprigs of chives
1 cup of Kyona Mustard Cress (Koppert Cress)

TECHNIQUES: GRILL, EMULSION, SOUR, RAW   **SUGGESTED BEVERAGE:** JOB BEER (BREWERY DE KROON, BELGIUM)

HAVE YOU EVER HEARD OF ARGAN OIL?

Among the biggest culinary discoveries made must be the discovery of argan oil! If you are not yet familiar with this product, you must know that argan oil isn't only healthy. It is above all a flavour carrier. Argan is a vegetable oil that comes from the fruit of the rare Argania spinosa, known as the tree of beauty. Fifteen years ago, hardly anyone outside Morocco knew about this Moroccan gold that Berber women were using for many centuries as their natural beauty product. The nutritional strengths of this oil are definitely its rich mix of fatty acids, antioxidants and vitamin E. In *Wild Cooking*, we only choose the premium quality of **Arqan.**

ADDED VALUE FOR LOCAL!

Local is the new normal these days! A good evolution that Wild Cooking also stands for. But what does local mean? For some it is his or her own garden, for others his or her country or continent. Does that mean we can't use spices, eat chocolate or drink coffee anymore? Of course we still can! The essence is that we buy locally what is available locally and at its best in the right season. And then there are products that can make a difference and that are worth having at home. The fantastic Moroccan Arqan oil is one of them. With a few drops of argan oil in or on your preparation, you travel the world!

WINTER

SWEET POTATO HUMMUS WITH SESAME CRACKERS AND CUZCO LEAVES

4 SERVINGS

 120 MINUTES    VEGGIES    LARGE DEEP BOWL (WILD MOON)

RECIPE

Chickpeas:
Soak chickpeas in 3 times the amount of water for 24 hours in the refrigerator.
Drain and rinse under cold running water.
Then bring to the boil in salted water with kafir lime leaves and a garlic clove.
Cover and simmer for up to 2 hours.
Allow to cool in the cooking liquid afterwards. Remove kafir leaves.

Sweet potato:
Peel the sweet potato and cut into pieces.
Cook in water with sea salt and garlic clove.

Hummus:
Finely chop a few of the Cuzco Leaves.
Blend this together with the chickpea, the warm sweet potato, some warm cooking liquid, black pepper, some za'atar and a good dash of olive oil to form a smooth mass.

Serve:
Place the hummus in a deep dish.
Finish with a few Cuzco Leaves, grilled sesame seeds, some extra za'atar and a few drops of argan oil.
Serve this together with the sesame crackers for dipping with an aperitif.

INGREDIENTS

1 teacup dried chickpeas
coarse sea salt (Verstegen)
2 kafir lime leaves
2 cloves of garlic
2 sweet potatoes
1 cup of Cuzco Leaves (Koppert Cress)
black pepper (Verstegen)
za'atar spice mix (Verstegen)
olive oil (Iluigi)
sesame seeds (Verstegen)
argan oil (Arqan)
sesame crackers

TECHNIQUES: STEW, EMULSION, RAW   **SUGGESTED BEVERAGE:** MARY V, TOMATO JUICE (NICK BRIL)

NUTRISCORE A

NUTRISCORE **A**

WINTER

ROASTED CHICKPEA CHERMOULA WITH BRIEFLY BRAISED ENDIVE, LEMON AND GANGNAM TOPS

4 SERVINGS

 120 MINUTES    VEGGIES    LARGE FLAT PLATE (WILD MOON)

RECIPE

Chickpea:
Soak chickpeas in 3 times the amount of water for 24 hours in the refrigerator. Drain and rinse under cold running water.
Then bring it to the boil in water with salt, bay leaf and garlic cloves.
Cook gently under the lid. This can take up to 2 hours.
Then let it cool in cooking liquid. Remove bay leaf.

Toasting:
Drain the chickpea and place in a pan with a dash of olive oil.
Season firmly with chermoula powder and some extra sea salt.
Stir-fry until light coloring on an (open) fire.

Endive:
Wash and cut endive into 4 cm pieces.
Stew these in some olive oil.
We make a warm salad, so the endive can shrink in a bit but it remains crispy.
Season well with sea salt, black pepper and grate some lemon zest over it.

Serve:
Divide the lukewarm endive on each plate.
Spoon the warm chickpeas over it.
Now drizzle some lemon juice, a few drops of olive oil from the pan over each preparation and decorate with a few sprigs of Gangnam Tops.
If necessary finish with a little chermoula powder.

TECHNIQUES: COOKING, ROASTING, BRAISING, RAW

SUGGESTED BEVERAGE: MARY V, TOMATO JUICE (NICK BRIL)

INGREDIENTS

tea cup dried chickpeas
coarse sea salt (Verstegen)
1 bay leaf (Verstegen)
2 garlic cloves
olive oil (Iluigi)
chermoula spice mix (Verstegen)
1 endive
black pepper (Verstegen)
juice and zest of 1 lemon
cup of Gangnam Tops (Koppert Cress)

NUTRISCORE **A**

WINTER

CHICORY POACHED IN ORANGE, PINE CONE, LIQUORICE, FRESH TARRAGON AND CLOVE BROTH

4 SERVINGS

 60 MINUTES    VEGGIES    FRUITS    LARGE FLAT PLATE (WILD MOON)

RECIPE

Ground chicory:
Clean and wash the chicory.
Prepare a broth with 3 pieces of orange zest, 2 cloves, a few pine cones, a stick of liquorice root, sea salt, black pepper, and a few sprigs of fresh tarragon.
Place the chicory in the broth, cover and poach. Pierce with knife to check for doneness. This can take up to 45 minutes.

Serve:
Spoon an abundant scoop of warm Légumaise artfully onto each plate.
Remove the chicory from the hot broth with a slotted spoon, dry on kitchen paper and place 1 in the centre of each plate. Dust with some sea salt and black pepper, then garnish with Kyona Mustard Cress, a sprig of tarragon and a few drops of olive oil and orange juice.

INGREDIENTS

4 sturdy heads of chicory
zest and juice from 1 orange
2 cloves (Verstegen)
some pine cones from the forest
(wash them before use)
1 stick of liquorice root
coarse sea salt (Verstegen)
black pepper (Verstegen)
fresh tarragon
150 g Bio Légumaise Amerika, pumpkin with orange
1 cup of Kyona Mustard Cress (Koppert Cress)
olive oil (Iluigi)

TECHNIQUES:
POACH, EMULSION, RAW

SUGGESTED BEVERAGE:
PINOT NOIR, PURE RED
(WINE CASTLE VANDEURZEN, BELGIUM)

WINTER

ROASTED WINTER CARROTS WITH CUMIN, RADISH SPROUTS AND HIPPO TOPS

4 SERVINGS

45 MINUTES VEGGIES LARGE FLAT PLATE (WILD MOON)

RECIPE

Carrot:
Peel and wash the carrots. Cut in half lengthwise.
Season well with sea salt, black pepper and cumin powder.
Now add some olive oil and pressed garlic. Mix everything well.
Place on the BBQ, not over full heat.
Grill for about 30 to 40 minutes. Turn regularly so they don't burn.

Serve:
Place a carrot half of both varieties on each plate.
Add 3 scoops of Légumaise.
Garnish with some radish sprouts and Hippo Tops.
Finish with a few drops of olive oil and some cumin powder.

INGREDIENTS

2 large yellow carrots
2 large purple carrots
coarse sea salt (Verstegen)
black pepper (Verstegen)
cumin powder (Verstegen)
olive oil (Iluigi)
2 garlic cloves
150 g Bio Légumaise Brabant, carrot with ginger
1 cup of purple radish sprouts
1 cup of Hippo Tops (Koppert Cress)

TECHNIQUES:
GRILL, EMULSION, RAW

SUGGESTED BEVERAGE:
GRÜNER VELTLINER, PURE WHITE
(WINE CASTLE VANDEURZEN, BELGIUM)

WINTER

RED CHICORY SALAD AND FRIED ORANGE SLICES WITH MIXED SPICE AND SHISO GREEN

4 SERVINGS

 20 MINUTES  VEGGIES  FRUITS  LARGE FLAT PLATE (WILD MOON)

RECIPE

Red chicory:
Clean and wash the red chicory. Loosen the leaves.

Orange:
Peel the oranges with a sharp knife.
Then cut crossways into slices of about 1 cm.
Splash some olive oil in a pan and put over the fire.
Place the slices in a hot pan and season with the mixed spice.
Fry very briefly, flipping the slices over after 1 minute using a turner.

Serve:
Place the lukewarm orange slices on the plates, alternating with the red chicory. Sprinkle with some mixed spice, black pepper and sea salt. Finish with the sprigs of Shiso Cress and a few drops of argan oil.

INGREDIENTS

4 heads of red chicory
4 oranges
olive oil (Iluigi)
mixed spice (Verstegen)
black pepper (Verstegen)
coarse sea salt (Verstegen)
1 cup of Shiso Green (Koppert Cress)
argan oil (Arqan)

TECHNIQUES:
FRY, RAW

SUGGESTED BEVERAGE:
ALBARIÑO, PURE WHITE (WINE CASTLE VANDEURZEN, BELGIUM)

NUTRISCORE A

NUTRISCORE **A**

WINTER

BRUSSELS SPROUTS SKEWER ON THE BBQ WITH APPLE-ELDERBERRY COMPOTE AND SCARLET CRESS

4 SERVINGS

 30 MINUTES    VEGGIES    FRUITS    LARGE FLAT PLATE (WILD MOON)

RECIPE

Brussels sprouts:
Clean and wash the sprouts.
Put them in a bowl and drizzle some argan oil on top and season with black pepper, mace powder and sea salt.
Now thread the sprouts onto the 4 skewers.
Grill over low heat for 15 to 20 minutes.
Turn regularly so that the Brussels sprouts are nicely browned all over but not burnt.

Compote:
Peel, core and dice the apples.
Cover and stew over low heat with 4 tablespoons of elderberry syrup.
When the apples are soft, blend everything into a smooth compote.

Serve:
Place compote in a jar or in the centre of a large plate.
Remove the Brussels sprouts from the skewers and serve cold or warm for dipping.
Garnish with some Scarlet Cress.

INGREDIENTS

500 g Brussels sprouts
argan oil (Arqan)
black pepper (Verstegen)
mace powder (Verstegen)
smoked sea salt (Verstegen)
2 stewing apples
4 tablespoons of elderberry syrup
1 cup of Scarlet Cress (Koppert Cress)
4 skewers

TECHNIQUES: GRILL, STEW, RAW

SUGGESTED BEVERAGE: DELVAUX BEER (BREWERY DE KROON, BELGIUM)

NUTRISCORE **A**

WINTER

BAKED POTATO WITH RAW JERUSALEM ARTICHOKE STRANDS, ARGAN OIL, CAVIAR AND PERSINETTE CRESS

4 SERVINGS

60 MINUTES   VEGGIES   LARGE DEEP PLATE (WILD MOON)

RECIPE

Potato:
Wash the potatoes. Place them over an outside fire (or in an oven) so that they can cook slowly without ending up in the flames and burning.
It can take up to 45 minutes for them to cook through.
Turn occasionally. Prick with a needle or knife to test if they are fully cooked.
Then cut the potatoes in half and spoon the insides out into a bowl.
Crush some with a fork and spoon and add the fresh cheese and a good dash of argan oil.
Season with sea salt and black pepper and mix well.
Fill the skins of the halved potatoes with this mixture.
Warm up again before serving.

Jerusalem artichoke:
Peel the Jerusalem artichoke.
Cut it into wafer-thin slices and then finely chop into threads.
Mix this with a few drops of argan oil and place a bunch on each potato half.

Serve:
Place 2 warm potato halves on each plate and top each one with a spoonful of caviar.
Dust with some freshly-ground black pepper and garnish with a few sprigs of Persinette Cress.

INGREDIENTS

4 medium-sized baking potatoes
4 tablespoons of fresh cheese
argan oil (Arqan)
coarse sea salt (Verstegen)
black pepper (Verstegen)
2 Jerusalem artichokes
160 g caviar
1 cup of Persinette Cress (Koppert Cress)

TECHNIQUES: GRILL, RAW

SUGGESTED BEVERAGE: CHARDONNAY PRESTIGE, PURE WHITE (WINE CASTLE VANDEURZEN, BELGIUM)

STEW POTS ARE BACK?

Stews are back in business! Is it nostalgia, convenience or just because stew dishes are really tasty and healthy? All of it! And they add to the core of cooking, the flavour! We are completely "wild" about the pots from **BergHOFF**, as you can see in our photos.

WINTER

PUMPKIN BLINIS WITH FRESH CHEESE AND MAOI CAVIAR

4 SERVINGS

 30 MINUTES    VEGGIES    LARGE FLAT PLATE (WILD MOON)

RECIPE

Pumpkin:
Peel and seed the pumpkin. Cube the flesh.
Cook in water with 1 sliced shallot.
When done, blend the pumpkin and shallot with a splash of cooking water and a dash of olive oil to a smooth, creamy paste.
Season well with some sea salt and black pepper.

Blinis:
Make a blini dough with some pumpkin paste.
Take 200 g of pumpkin paste. Beat the eggs lightly and add milk, flour and baking powder. Now mix with pumpkin and season with salt and pepper.
Heat some olive oil in a frying pan. Add batter by the tablespoon and fry small blinis, turn so that they are nicely baked on both sides.
Finish batter and keep blinis warm.

Shallot:
Finely chop shallot.

Serve:
Spoon an oval of warm pumpkin paste onto each warm plate.
Top each with 2 warm blinis. Top with a spoonful of fresh cheese and season with black pepper and place a few Moai Caviar strands on each blini.
Now sprinkle with the chopped shallot and serve.

INGREDIENTS

1 small straight butternut squash
2 shallots
olive oil (Iluigi)
coarse sea salt (Verstegen)
black pepper (Verstegen)
2 eggs
250 ml of whole milk
150 g spelt flour
1 tsp baking powder
4 tablespoons of fresh cheese
jar of Moai Caviar (Koppert Cress)

TECHNIQUES: FRY, RAW, EMULSION

SUGGESTED BEVERAGE: CHARDONNAY, PURE WHITE (WINE CASTLE VANDEURZEN, BELGIUM)

NUTRISCORE **A**

THE CERAMICS PROCESS

Have you ever wondered how clays become ceramics? Making ceramics is a very long process. Not only are you limited in how many pieces you can turn in a day, but you should only fire your kiln once you've turned about 100 of them. And then the pieces are fired in the kiln twice over the course of two days. Thankfully, it's worth the wait.

KNEADING
Each piece of clay should be kneaded about 60 times to remove any air and to make the clay nice and smooth.

WEIGHING
The clay should be weighed to achieve the desired shape.

TURNING
Put your clay on the potter's wheel and start turning!

SHAPING
Shape the clay into whatever shape you like: plate, a mug, a bowl…

TRIMMING
Let the clay dry until it is leather-hard. Then you can trim your work. Tweak it into its final shape.

STAMPING
Make the shape nice and smooth and then mark your work with a stamp.

DRYING
Leave the clay to dry for a week.

BISCUIT FIRING
Once the work is dry, it is fired for 36 hours in the kiln at 950 degrees. This is called biscuit firing. The shape shrinks by about 10% during this process.

GLAZE FIRING
The cups and plates are then glazed and returned to the oven for another 36 hours at 1240 degrees. This also makes them dishwasher safe. The shape shrinks slightly during this stage.

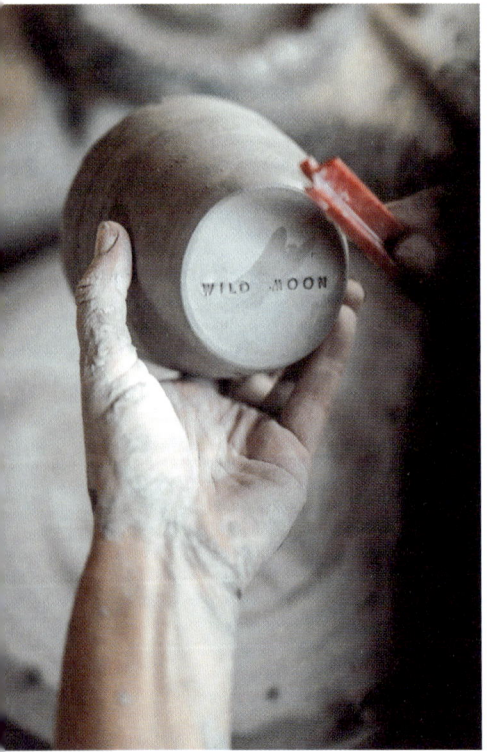

NUTRISCORE **A**

WINTER

GRILLED WINTER LEEK WITH BEETROOT-PEAR COULIS, PUFFED BLACK RICE AND SCARLET CRESS

4 SERVINGS

 45 MINUTEN (BUITEN DE RIJST)    VEGGIES    LARGE FLAT PLATE (WILD MOON)

RECIPE

Leek:
Clean and wash leek. May be placed whole on the grill over coals, not flame. Cook slowly, turning occasionally.
Can take up to 45 minutes.

Coulis:
Peel the pear and core it. Cut into pieces and gently simmer with a dash of olive oil and moisten with a good dash of the beer. When the pear is cooked, blend everything together with the cooked beetroot (peeled) to form a smooth, thick sauce.
Season with a little curry powder and sea salt.

Puffing the black rice:
Cook the rice until tender.
Drain and then spread it out on a baking tray.
Dry it in an oven at 120 °C for 2 to 3 hours.
Have a metal slotted spoon and a paper towel ready.
Now fry the dried rice in a pot with about 3 cm groundnut or rice oil. You can check the temperature of the hot oil by throwing in a grain as a test; if it pops up, you can add all the rice.
This happens very quickly. It is ready in a few seconds and you scoop out all the rice grains and put them on the kitchen paper.
Season with a little salt. You can also buy puffed rice if this is more convenient.

Serve:
Cut large pieces of the leek.
Cut it in half and place warm on each plate.
Spoon some sauce on the side. Garnish with the puffed rice, Scarlet Cress and dust with some extra curry powder.

INGREDIENTS

2 pieces of leek
1 ripe pear of your choice
olive oil (Iluigi)
bottle of strong blond Belgian beer (Brewery De Kroon)
100 g cooked beetroot
curry powder (Verstegen)
coarse sea salt (Verstegen)
4 tablespoons of black rice
1 cup of Scarlet Cress (Koppert Cress)

TECHNIQUES: GRILL, PUFF, SAUCE, RAW   **SUGGESTED BEVERAGE:** SUPER KROON BEER (BREWERY DE KROON, BELGIUM)

NUTRISCORE **A**

WINTER

PEAR COMPOTE WITH GINGER AND TURMERIC, NOCCIOLA OLIVE ICE CREAM, ROASTED HAZELNUT AND YKA LEAVES

4 SERVINGS

 30 MINUTES    VEGGIES    FRUITS   NUTS    SMALL BOWL (WILD MOON)

RECIPE

Compote:
Peel a 4 cm piece of ginger and grate or chop finely. Peel and core pears. Cut into pieces and simmer gently with the ginger, a teaspoon of turmeric powder and a dash of olive oil, cover and cook until it forms a compote. Cool in the refrigerator.

Serve:
Spoon some compote into each bowl. Spoon a scoop of the Iluigi nocciola ice cream on top and garnish with chopped, roasted hazelnuts, a few drops of olive oil and some finely chopped Yka Leaves.

INGREDIENTS

piece of fresh ginger
4 ripe pears
1 tsp turmeric powder (Verstegen)
olive oil (Iluigi)
nocciola ice cream (Iluigi)
roasted hazelnuts
1 cup of Yka Leaves (Koppert Cress)

TECHNIQUES:
COMPOTE, RAW, ICE CREAM, ROAST, BOUILLON

SUGGESTED BEVERAGE:
FRESH GINGER TEA (HOT OR COLD)

WINTER

OPEN PUMPKIN RAVIOLI WITH ACHELSE BLUE CRUMBLE, PARSLEY SAUCE AND YKA LEAVES

4 SERVINGS

 30 MINUTES    VEGGIES    LARGE FLAT PLATE (WILD MOON)

RECIPE

Mince:

Take a piece of pumpkin and peel it. Using a mandoline, make 3 long thin strips of about 14 cm by 4 cm, for each person.
Finely mince the less beautiful pumpkin pieces.
Also peel and finely chop the shallot.
Gently simmer the shallot and pumpkin mince with a dash of olive oil, don't brown.
Season well with black pepper, sea salt and some mace powder.
Now finely chop a sprig of curly parsley and mix into the mince.

Ravioli:

Briefly cook the 12 slices of pumpkin in boiling water with sea salt (about 30 seconds) and transfer to a towel or kitchen paper.

Sauce:

Wash a handful of curly parsley and drop briefly into the warm cooking water from the pumpkin. Let it boil for a while and scoop out with the help of a slotted spoon.
Puree the parsley with a good splash of cooking water and olive oil.
Season well with sea salt and black pepper to form a smooth, spicy green sauce.

Serve:

Preheat plates. Put together 3 raviolis on each plate by filling each pumpkin strip with a spoonful of warm mince.
Now spoon some green sauce onto the plates, crumble some blue cheese, drizzle some olive oil and garnish with the Yka Leaves.

INGREDIENTS

small straight butternut squash
1 shallot
olive oil (Iluigi)
black pepper (Verstegen)
coarse sea salt (Verstegen)
mace powder (Verstegen)
bunch of curly parsley
120 g Achel blue cheese
1 cup of Yka Leaves (Koppert Cress)

TECHNIQUES: COOK, STEW, MINCE, RAW, SAUCE

SUGGESTED BEVERAGE: CUVÉE PURE RED (WINE CASTLE VANDEURZEN, BELGIUM)

NUTRISCORE **A**

WINTER

YELLOW BEETROOT ROLLS WITH SHIITAKE-HAZELNUT FILLING, LÉGUMAISE TRUFFLE AND RUCOLACRESS

4 SERVINGS

 30 MINUTES  VEGGIES   NUTS  LARGE FLAT PLATE (WILD MOON)

RECIPE

Beet:
Peel and wash the beets.
Cut in half and use a mandolin to make fine, thin round slices on the largest side, 3 to 5 per person.
Immerse them very briefly (max. 30 seconds) in boiling water with sea salt.
Scoop out and cool in ice water.

Mince:
Make the mince with the remaining beets (2/5), the shitake mushrooms (2/5) and some hazelnuts (1/5) into small pieces.
Stew everything together until crisp with some olive oil.
Season with a little thyme, black pepper and sea salt.

Rolls:
Now scoop a spoonful of mince onto each slice of beet and roll into equal rolls.
Place these together on a plate and heat up in the microwave before serving.

Serve:
Place an oval of Légumaise in each plate and place the rolls next to each other.
Garnish with a few drops of argan oil and some Arugula Cress.

TECHNIQUES: COOK, STEW, MINCE, RAW, EMULSION

SUGGESTED BEVERAGE: CHARDONNAY PRESTIGE, PURE WHITE (WINE CASTLE VANDEURZEN, BELGIUM)

INGREDIENTS

2 large yellow beets
coarse sea salt (Verstegen)
200 g shiitake mushrooms
roasted hazelnuts
olive oil (Iluigi)
dried thyme (Verstegen)
black pepper (Verstegen)
Bio Légumaise mushroom with truffle
argan oil (Arqan)
1 cup of RucolaCress (Koppert Cress)

NUTRISCORE A

WE'RE SMART® WORLD RECOGNISED BY FIDO!

Thee **SDG Voices** for 2021 are known. SDG stands for "Sustainable Development Goals" that the UN has set to improve the world. The Belgian Federal Institute for Sustainable Developments (FIDO) recently announced the new Belgian voices. We're Smart® World can now call itself SDG Voice. There are 17 goals that are being worked around with the aim of improving or achieving them by 2030. We're Smart® will mainly focus on the following goals:

- **Good health and well-being (Goal 3):** focus on vegetables and fruits.
- **Quality education (Goal 4):** the right support and training in the We're Smart® Academy.
- **Responsible consumption & production (Goal 12):** support for innovation in food.
- **Partnership to achieve goals (Goal 17):** join forces with like-minded people and promote healthy innovative products and projects.
- **Of course we also fully support the other SDG objectives!**

We're Smart® World also wants to contribute to sustainable developments in Belgium and in the world! Long live the future!

INDEX

Aclla Cress 92
Adji Cress 144
Almonds 139
Anise Blossom 147
Apple Blossom 111
Apple vinegar 164
Apricots 99, 139
Argan oil 46, 57, 61, 72, 79, 83, 89, 90, 125, 126, 135, 144, 159, 164, 170, 178, 181, 185, 198
Asparagus, green 130
Asparagus, white 58, 74
Baking powder 79, 188
Basil, Thai 57, 107
Basilicum 139
Bay leaf 161, 173
Beer, Super Kroon 89, 135
Beet, red 79, 193
Beet, yellow 198
Bio Légumaise Amerika, pumpkin with orange 175
Bio Légumaise Bilbao, yellow paprika with lemon 104
Bio Légumaise Brabant, carrot with ginger 25, 176
Bio Légumaise Italia, tomato with basil 42, 144
Bio Légumaise Périgord, mushroom with truffle 37, 126, 198
Bio Légumaise Provence, paprika with thyme 92, 115
Bio Légumaise Thai, red curry with coconut 34, 57
Bio Légumaise Vietnam, celeriac with curry 125, 152
Blue cheese, Achel 196
Bread, pumpernickel 161
Bread, toasted 100
Bread, wholemeal 29, 37
Broccoli 139
Buckwheat, roasted 144
Burrata 92
Butter 58, 79, 125, 135, 149, 161

Butternut squash 188, 196
Cabbage, pointed 57, 61
Cabbage, red 161
Cabbage, white 161
Cane sugar 79
Carrot 25, 130
Carrots, purple 176
Carrots, yellow 90, 176
Cashew nuts 61, 125
Cauliflower 24, 74, 152
Cauliflower, purple 126, 146
Caviar 58, 83, 149, 185
Cayenne pepper 30, 89, 149, 152
Celeriac root 159
Celery sticks 25
Celery, green 121
Celery, white 149
Celery, white 42
Cheese, Brugge Oud 125, 139
Cheese, Flandrien Oud 37
Cheese, fresh 185, 188
Chermoula 51, 173
Cherries 111
Cherry tomatoes 85, 147
Chervil 90
Chestnut mushrooms 121, 135
Chickpeas, dried 170, 173
Chicory 175
Chicory, red 178
Chili, red 107, 130
Chives 152, 164
Chives, fresh 152
Chocolate, black 79, 112
Citra Leaves 125
Clove 175
Coriander 34
Courgette, green 140
Courgette, yellow 100
Crackers 25
Crackers, sesame 170
Cranberries 159
Cranberries, dried 159
Crema di tartufi bianci 74
Cucumber 30, 95, 107

Cucumber, baby 152
Cumin powder 30, 176
Curry powder 193
Cuzco Leaves 170
Daikon Cress 135
Dill 85, 147
Eggs 42, 79, 188
Elderberry syrup 181
Endive 173
Fennel 34, 67, 85
Flax seeds 115
Floregano 29
Flour 41
Flower, spelt 188
Gangnam Topps 173
Garden Cress 37
Garlic 30, 41, 121, 125, 135, 161, 170, 173, 176
Ghoa Cress 34, 90, 159
Ginger nut biscuits 71
Ginger, fresh 34, 130, 140, 195
Goat cheese 69, 77, 144, 149
Goji berries 67
Gomasio 64, 159
Grapefruit, pink 67, 159
Grapes, green 147
Hazelnut 126, 161, 195, 198
Hippo Tops 89, 176
Honey 71, 111
Honey, truffle 77
Honny Cress 71
Jasmine Blossom 126, 139
Jerusalem artichokes 185
Kafir lime leaves 170
Kefir 30
Kikuna Leaves 25
Kohlrabi 126
Kyona Mustard Cress 61, 164, 175
Lavender 99
Leek 41, 83, 104, 193
Lemon balm 111
Lemon verbena 95, 115
Lemon, juice of 72, 85, 95, 139, 173

INDEX

Lemon, zest of 95, 100, 115, 139, 173
Lime, juice of 24, 34, 90, 107, 130, 147
Limon Cress 46, 99, 112, 132, 140
Liquorice root 175
Lupine Cress 161
Mace powder 29, 58, 61, 83, 125, 161, 164, 181, 196
Mangetout 77
Mango 34
Marjoram 83, 92
Melissa Cress 30
Milk, whole 188
Mint, fresh 24
Mitsuna lettuce 57
Mixed spice 178
Moai Caviar 188
Motti Cress 25, 100, 121
Mozzzarella 104
Nocciola ice cream 195
Nori, sheet of 90
Oatmeal 24
Olive ice cream 71, 95
Olive oil 22, 28, 30, 33, 37, 45, 53, 59, 75, 77, 84, 87, 91, 92, 96, 99, 108, 112, 115, 121, 130, 139, 140, 147, 152, 159, 170, 173, 175, 176, 178, 188, 193, 195, 196, 198
Olives, green 92
Onion 30, 41, 51, 83
Onion, red 37, 139
Onion, white 89
Oranges 175, 178
Oyster Leaves 149
Parsley, curly 25, 196
Pasta, rigatoni 139
Pastry flour 79
Pattypan, mini 104
Pazztiz Tops 72
Peaches 51
Peanuts, roasted 107
Pears 67, 193, 195
Peas 41

Pepper, black 25, 41, 42, 46, 51, 58, 61, 64, 67, 83, 85, 90, 92, 100, 104, 115, 121, 125, 126, 135, 139, 144, 147, 159, 161, 164, 170, 173, 175, 176, 178, 181, 188, 196, 19
Persilette 74, 185
Pine cones 175
Pistachio ice cream 140
Pistachio nuts 67, 140
Potato, sweet 41, 147, 170
Potatoes, soft boiling 46, 51, 58, 161, 185
Potatoes, waxy 121, 149
Quark 111
Quinoa 57
Radish sprouts, purple 176
Radish, white 135, 144
Radishes 34, 37, 61
Rapeseed flowers 115
Rapeseed oil 126
Ras el hanout 130
Raspberries 46, 95
Raspberry vinegar 46
Red bell pepper 34, 92, 134
Redcurrants 64
Rhubarb stalks 71, 72
Rice, black 193
Rosemary 159
RucolaCress 58, 74, 198
Salsa tartufata 74
Savory 125, 135
Scarlet Cress 181, 193
Sea fennel 41, 85
Sea salt 24, 30, 34, 42, 51, 57, 64, 67, 83, 85, 89, 90, 92, 107, 112, 121, 125, 126, 130, 152, 159, 161, 164, 170, 173, 175, 176, 178, 185, 188, 193, 196, 198
Sea salt, smoked 41, 61, 181
Sesame seeds 57, 90, 147, 170
Shallot 25, 41, 47, 107, 125, 126, 152, 188, 196
Shiitake 125, 198

Shiso Green Cress 178
Shiso Leaves Green 42
Spaghetti 100
Spinach 37, 85, 100
Spring onion 115
Sprouts, Brussels 181
Stewing apples 29, 181
Strawberries 72, 140
Sunflower seeds 130
Swiss chard stalk 51, 125
Syrha Leaves 107
Tarragon 175
Tea, loose 90
Tempranillo, red wine 64
Thyme 104
Thyme, dried 198
Tomatoes, beef 29
Truffle oil, white 42
Truffle powder 29
Truffle sea salt, white 37
Turmeric powder 152, 195
Turnip 24
Turnips 64, 83, 164
Turnips, spring 64
Vanilla powder 79
Vene Cress 51
Watercress 89
Watermelon 24, 85
White wine vinegar 30, 144
Wild garlic 100
Yellow sweet pepper 92
Yka Leaves 67, 195, 196
Yogurt 99
Yogurt, Greek 24
Za'atar 170

WILD COOKING IS ALL ABOUT 'TOGETHER WE ARE STRONG'!

We believe that in these challenging times there is more need for togetherness. We support sustainable cooperations, simply because they are so much stronger. By working together, we can all jump further, can't we? That is why we are pleased to say that these partners have supported the 'Wild Cooking' initiative. We would like to thank them for their confidence and their contribution to the success of this story.

The Vegetables Chef Frank Fol, for the delicious recipes
www.weresmartworld.com

Ilse De Vis of Wild Moon Ceramics, for the presentation in natural ceramics
www.wildmoon.be

Wim Demessemaekers of Soul Food Photographer, for the authentic photography
www.soulfoodphotographer.com
www.soulfoodrevolution.com
www.atasteoftanzania.com

Verstegen Spices & Sauces, for the best herbs and spices
www.verstegen.be

BergHoff kitchen utensils and cookware, for the quality knives and stew pots
www.berghoffworldwide.com

Iluigi, for the organic extra virgin olive oil and the ice cream made from olive oil
www.iluigi.be

Koppert Cress, for the innovative and tasty mini vegetables
www.koppertcress.com

Ekomenu, for the tasty balanced ECO meals
www.ekomenu.be

Légumaise, for the most delicious vegetable sauces
www.weresmartworld.com/legumaise

Brewery De Kroon, for the right choice of beers
www.brouwerijdekroon.be

Arqan Oil, for the pure and organic culinary argan oil
www.arqanoil.com

SDG Voices
www.sdgs.be/en/sdg-voices